CW01263103

Silver Link Silk Editions

SLP

One young lad's later trainspotting trips with a camera, 1961-1964

Previous page: With what appeared to be no single strategic plan in terms of motive power from the British Railways Board, the Western Region went its own way in 1958 and introduced diesel-hydraulic locomotives, initially with the 'Warship' Class. However, in 1967 BR's hierarchy decided that the design was non-standard to its future plan, and the locomotives should all be withdrawn – what a waste of investment! Here we see No D817 *Foxhound* approaching Newton Abbot; she was only in service for 11 years, eventually being cut up at her birthplace of Swindon. (28 August 1963)

Above: In this view from the western side of Newton Abbot station, North British diesel-hydraulic Type 2 No D6332, after having passed the power station on the left and the sheds, works and carriage yards partially visible on the right, departs with a local to Dartmouth. It is passing what then was the offices of publishers David & Charles on the right. (26 August 1963)

Silver Link Silk Editions

SLP

One young lad's later trainspotting trips with a camera, 1961-1964

Alan M. Clarke

Silver Link Books

© Alan M. Clarke 2021

All rights reserved. No part of this publication may be reproduced, stored in a retrieval system or transmitted, in any form or by any means, electronic, mechanical, photocopying, recording or otherwise, without prior permission in writing from Silver Link Books, Mortons Media Group Ltd.

First published in 2021

British Library Cataloguing in Publication Data

A catalogue record for this book is available from the British Library.

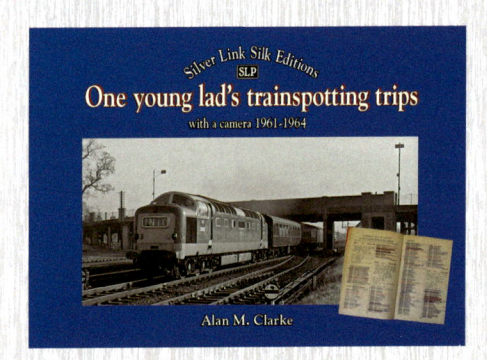

ISBN 978 1 85794 555 3

Silver Link Books
Mortons Media Group Limited
Media Centre
Morton Way
Horncastle
LN9 6JR
Tel/Fax: 01507 529535

email: sohara@mortons.co.uk
Website: www.nostalgiacollection.com

Printed and bound in the Czech Republic

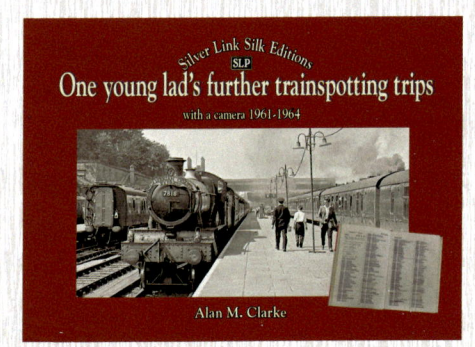

The first volume ISBN: 978 1 85794 472 3

The second volume ISBN: 978 1 85794 541 0

Contents

Introduction	5
1 The English Riviera	9
2 Barry and Woodhams	24
3 Severn Tunnel Junction, Newport and Cardiff	35
4 Stockport and Bolton	52
5 The Glasgow area	60
6 The North East	71
7 The Swansea area	83
8 The Birmingham area	94
9 The Leeds area	112
Index	127

Dedication

'No llores porque ya se terminó, sonríe porque sucedió'
'Don't, cry because it's over, smile because it happened'
Gabriel Garcia Marquez

Chris, thanks for the memories
Love Alan xxx

Introduction

'Sometimes you will never know the value of a moment, until it becomes a memory.'
Georges Duhamel, *The Heart's Domain*, 1919

In the 1950s and early 1960s the hobby of trainspotting was infectious, almost reaching epidemic proportions, particularly with boys. I was one who was immediately hooked, after just seeing one Brunswick Green 'Pacific' pass by. It was Class 'A3' No 60056 *Centenary* at Retford, and my first impressions were 'Wow – I want some more of that!' That first experience took me on a six-year journey from 1958 to 1964, covering most of the spotting hotspots around the country, initially just taking numbers then for the last four years also taking photographs.

Sometimes when you look back on your life you wonder what it would have been like to have been born 10 or 20 years earlier, and in respect of this hobby it would probably have been a good thing, giving more time to complete your sets of locomotives. The reality is that, in my opinion, if you were born earlier the pros were far outweighed by the cons – quoting from Dickens's *A Tale of Two Cities*, 'It was the best of times, it was the worst of times.'

Born earlier I would have been exposed to a war-torn Britain and all the consequences: poverty, rationing, family members killed in action, exposure to certain medical ailments that are now either controllable or eradicated – the list goes on, with not many plusses in my opinion. So really I am glad I was born in 1948; rationing would soon to be over, conscription ended in 1960, groceries were sold in brown paper bags, and beer was served from oak casks, in the main 36-gallon barrels with sediment that needed about two days to settle before it could be served. Today's real ale gangs are convinced that what is on offer today is the best – there's really no contest. We are all biased towards the decade that we became interested in music; for me the 1960s were the best, groups revolutionising the industry with new beats, melodies, sounds, fashion, involvement and happiness. In the music industry it almost seemed that if you could sing and came from Liverpool you couldn't fail.

In education O-Levels were the qualification to have, but now they have been eroded with A-Level passes being the prerequisite for university entry. For my part, schooling was over at 15, and university didn't seem to be a topic of discussion; now it is almost obligatory, and in some instances the debt far outweighs the benefits from the qualification gained. Having said all that, I now probably belong to the 'grumpy old fart' brigade, and occasionally my daughter Zoe in conversation drops the Victor Meldrew comment! I say nothing but think 'Wait until you are 72, then reflect back!'

But our experiences gained over our lifespan have to be recorded, otherwise they will eventually be lost for ever. How many times have you heard, 'My gran used to cook this meal and it was unbelievable but now she's passed away the recipe and method have gone with her, lost for ever.' Well, in that respect it was one of the reasons for me to record my trainspotting experiences for now and future reading and reference. My memory is still good and, in respect of my hobby, is vivid, so while that remains the case I will carry on. They say publishing is the first draft to history.

I have mentioned before that the availability of information in the early 1960s, other than the main current news items, was to me non-existent. With no internet searching available, the monthly railway periodicals were the best you could get, but even they were a few weeks out of date by the time you read them. I spent a week at my auntie's in Grantham during the summer holidays in 1960 and was amazed to see so many trains coming in, stopping and having a change of engine. To see 'A4s', 'A3s', 'A2s' and 'A1s' pulling off a train and going light engine to the shed with another one backing on to me was mesmerising. I really had no idea why this was happening. I know now it was mainly to do with the logistics of the locomotives and the

One young lad's later trainspotting trips

Western and Southern Regions, all addressed to the Traffic Manager at the addresses in the passenger timetables for that region (not knowing anything different), enquiring about the availability of nameplates. The only way you were able to keep a copy of your letter was to use carbon paper, and since I didn't have any I only have the replies, and it was evident from them that my letters had been redirected to the appropriate department.

The figures that British Railways was asking for nameplates was frightening and prohibitive for me, 15 years old and earning £3 2s 6d a week – no chance. This called for a rethink and I decided to write again and ask for the prices of numberplates and worksplates. After a look in the current month's *Trains Illustrated* at what had been withdrawn, I selected a few locos and enquired about availability. Replies took a good few days, but no luck, as my selections had already been sold – another example of outdated information. My next enquiries were for general availability, and this proved to be the best tactic with replies coming from the North Eastern and Western Regions, listing what was available at the time of writing. I selected a brass worksplate available at Darlington from Class 'D49' No 62765 *The Goathland*, priced at 10 shillings delivered by rail, and a cast cabside from Swindon off Class '4500' No 5534 at 5 shillings, also delivered by rail. I remember the cabside plate being delivered by a British Railway van driver; it came in a hessian sack with a tie-on label, looking similar to a cartoonist's portrayal of a burglar's 'swag bag'!

crews, but if I had known that then I might have realised that on the up trains from Edinburgh the same thing in reverse was happening at Newcastle, and a visit there would possibly have cleared up all my Scottish 'Pacifics' – a complete lack of working knowledge for which I paid the price of incomplete sets!

With usually about 100 locos being withdrawn every month, I decided to investigate buying some railway memorabilia after aborted attempts to relieve engines of their name, number and works plates due to only having a pair of pliers. I sent letters to the Eastern,

About a week after receiving the brass plate from Darlington and over a period of two weeks I received two letters from the accounts section asking for payment. Each time I replied stating that I had paid and quoting my postal order receipt number. I didn't hear any more so I assume they traced payment – or did they? Fortunately, I kept all the correspondence from British Railways in respect of the two plates because, as they say on *Antiques Roadshow*, it's all about provenance.

To complement the worksplate I bought a Hornby OO gauge model of Class 'D49' No 62750 *The Pytchley* and had it renumbered and renamed to represent No 62765 *The Goathland*.

Taking numbers by the lineside and on station platforms was good, but you could get a lot more by going around the sheds and works, and for all the trespassing I did the success rate was very high. But underlining in my 'ABC' needed another boost, so I progressed to organised coach trips, a one-dayer doing maybe

Introduction

Taken from the Torquay Road overbridge at Newton Abbot we see 'Hall' Class No 5992 *Horton Hall*. She performed regularly on the hourly services between Newton Abbot and Paignton and return all week, and here she is coasting into the station having joined the main line from Plymouth half a mile earlier at Aller Junction. (26 August 1963)

ten sheds. I quickly realised that this was the way forward in order to see as many locos as I could before the end. Although I knew the end was close, until it happened I never thought it would; as Yogi Berra (the American baseball catcher, not the cartoon character) said, 'It ain't over till it's over.'

Reflecting on the trips now, I am amazed how the coach drivers drove for about 10 hours and arrived at the entrances of maybe ten sheds just aided by a road map and prompts from senior members of the party. I was never aware of the driver having to reverse out of a situation because he had gone the wrong way – a really good effort that I don't suppose was ever recognised and appreciated at the time by us youngsters. And since we had never been abroad for our holidays we had never been exposed or introduced to tipping, so they got nothing!

The majority of the photographs included in this book – the third in the series – were taken in the leap year of 1964, a year that gave us the Beatles appearing on *The Ed Sullivan Show* in America with an estimated audience of 73 million, Cassius Clay beating Sonny Liston, Nelson Mandela starting his life sentence, Mary Poppins coming into our lives, the release of *Goldfinger*, the Shinkansen high-speed rail system, *Top of the Pops* and *Match of the Day*. What an eventful year!

I hope you enjoy the following photos and captions, which provide a record of my railway events of the day, thankfully recorded.

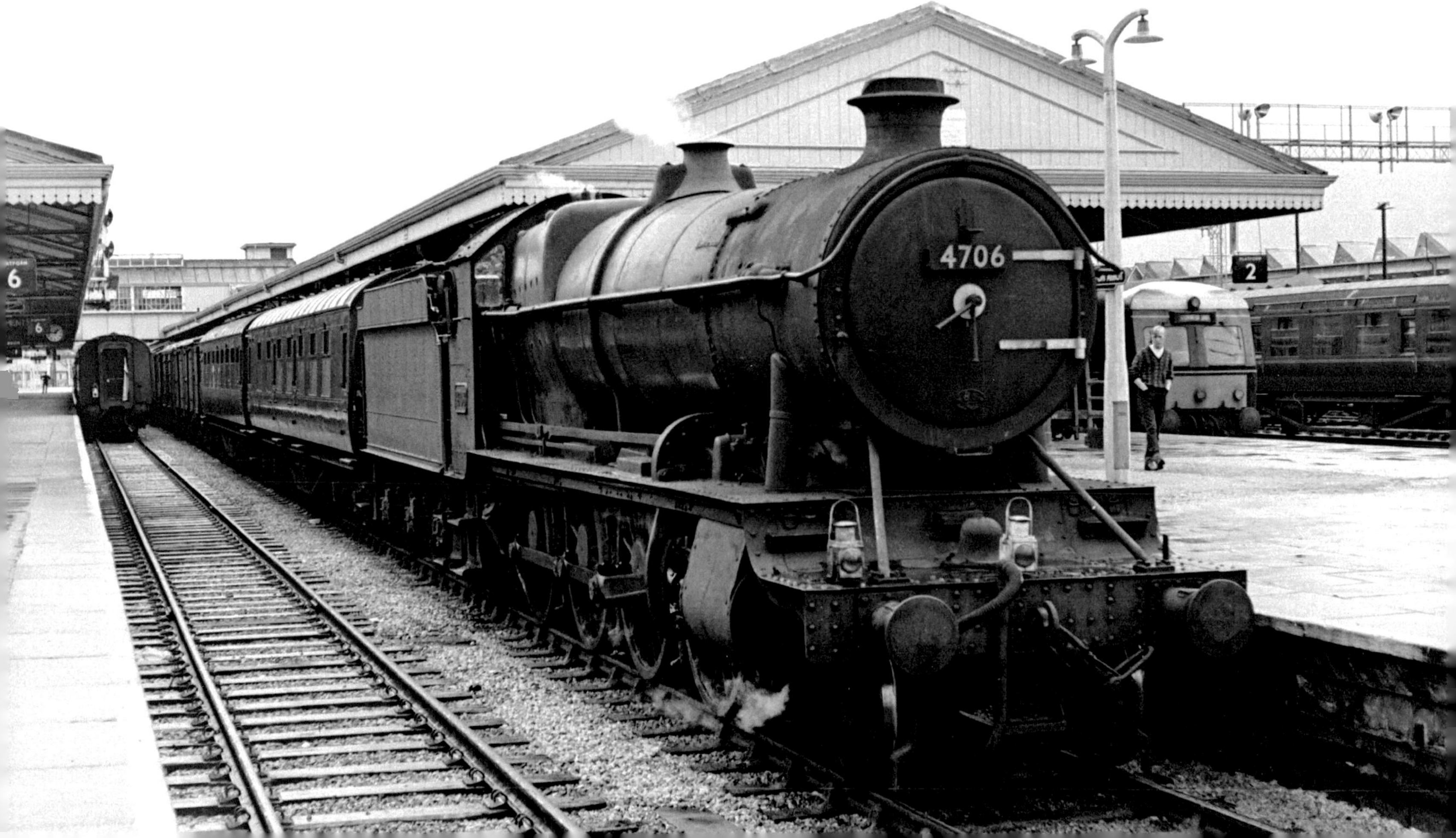
6
4706
2

1 • The English Riviera

Renowned for its mild climate, beautiful coastal areas and vegetation (palm trees), this holiday destination area has since Victorian times adopted the name of 'the English Riviera'. Tourism is the main industry in the region and in 1998 it became the Unitary Authority of Torbay, with responsibility for its own affairs. I was fortunate to go there on holiday in 1963 when I was 15 with a trainspotting mate Geoffrey – 'Jaffa' – and his Mam and Dad, who used to have the local Co-op store. We travelled from Worksop in an Aqua Blue Ford Anglia, the journey taking a cramped, hot 8 hours, although these days a clear run of 4½ hours is possible. Jaffa's interest in trainspotting was, I think, beginning to wane, but I was still totally committed and couldn't get enough. It was a bit fortuitous really, because our first day was spent on the beach and Jaffa got very burned in the sun, to such an extent that he did not want to do it again, so for the rest of the week we went spotting, with Jaffa smelling of calamine lotion and itching.

For me, not knowing a lot about the area at that time, it turned out to be great for railway photography, all along the coast with a different setting around each corner. Not having done the usual Beattock and Shap locations, this for me was the best. Steam was on the decline and the trains were predominantly diesel-hauled, but as I have said before everything has its place in history and should be respected.

Left: The '4700' Class 2-8-0s were primarily designed for heavy freight working, and Nos 4706 and 4707, although still sporting 81C Southall shedplates, somehow found their way down to the West Country and worked passenger duties to Plymouth and Penzance. Here we see No 4706 at Newton Abbot about to depart. We were listening to *Rhythm of the Rain* by the Cascades, although it wasn't actually cascading down, but more of a drizzle! (28 August 1963)

Right: I'm on my way to Newton Abbot, being pulled by a 'Hall', and an unidentified North British Type 2 diesel-hydraulic is coming in the opposite direction. I am performing the dangerous 'head out of the window' shot, taboo in today's health and safety environment. Note the verandas on the houses, which are a common feature on properties on the English Riviera. (28 August 1963)

Below: 'NOTT BRODIE'. Who is it then? It's 'Warship' Class No D824 *Highflyer* travelling light to the carriage sidings at Newton Abbot. *Highflyer* entered service in July 1960 and was withdrawn in December 1972 with 1,077,000 miles on the clock, eventually being cut up at Swindon in 1975. (26 August 1963)

Above: An unidentified 'Hall' double-heads with 'Warship' Class No D848 *Sultan* with a train bound for Penzance, maybe doubled-headed to assist when attacking Dainton Bank just past Aller Junction. With a gradient varying between 1 in 36 and 1 in 57, it is the third steepest bank on the British Railway system. (28 August 1963)

Below: One of the original 'Hall' Class, No 4903 *Astley Hall*, built in 1928 and named after a country house near Stourport-on-Severn that was home to Prime Minister Stanley Baldwin for 45 years, is seen here approaching Newton Abbot. (28 August 1963)

Above: North British Type 2 No D6333, double-heading with an unidentified 'Warship' Class, awaits a 3.13pm departure from Newton Abbot to Dartmouth with its three coaches. Platform 1 looks incredibly clean and tidy, but then again there are five railway officials there to make sure everything is in place. On the right you can see the lighting gantries over the carriage sidings, to enable cleaning to continue throughout the night. Note the different font on the 'Refreshments' sign. (28 August 1963)

One young lad's later trainspotting trips

Left: The shadows lengthen in the early evening sun as Beyer Peacock Type 3 ('Hymek') No D7001 stops alongside the signal box at Torquay with a rake of ten coaches, next stop Paignton. The car park is full of late 1950s and early 1960s car designs, and a billboard advertises John Courage and Guinness adjacent to the pretty, well-kept station. (28 August 1963)

Right: Old meets new, and again we see No 5992 *Horton Hall* as she enters Torquay from Newton Abbot with 'Warship' No D832 *Onslaught* awaiting departure in the opposite direction. Visible on the extreme left is a platform that was used primarily for loading goods, and has one of the old loading gauges at the end. (28 August 1963)

Right: Another view of 'Warship' No D832 *Onslaught* at Torquay, having stopped adjacent to the bay platforms on the right that were normally used for postal and parcels traffic, but also possessed an end-loading facility, which was especially convenient for the unloading of animals during the annual visit to the town of Bertram Mills Circus (according to Roy Hobbs's book *Working Steam: Collett Castles and Kings*, page 34). The large guesthouse-looking properties on the hill to the right are all typical of Basil and Sybil's 'Fawlty Towers'! (28 August 1963)

Left: An unidentified 'Warship' Class approaches Torquay passing under the triple-span Seaway Lane overbridge. Today the two side arches are obscured by tree growth, the crossover between the two tracks has been removed and the 'Warship' has gone. (28 August 1963)

Clean but not shining is 'Hall Class No 5992 *Horton Hall* at Paignton, attracting interest from four spotters who appear to be forming a queue to talk to the driver; the little boy in the middle, with his summer shorts and sandals, is waiting patiently. (28 August 1963)

The English Riviera

With the south level crossing gates at Sands Road open and the typical Great Western lower-quadrant signal indicating proceed, an unidentified 'Hall' Class departs from Paignton for Dartmouth. Although there wasn't a station at Dartmouth, you could book a through ticket, disembark at Kingswear and catch the ferry.
(28 August 1963)

In this view from the other end of Paignton station looking towards Torbay Road, the crossing gates are closed and North British-built 'Warship' Class No D847 *Strongbow*, with the usual three-coach local train, awaits departure. She was built in 1961, and coincidentally Bulmer's had introduced its 'Strongbow' cider in 1960 – so was she named after a naval ship or the cider? (28 August 1963)

Right: 'Hall' Class No 4914 *Cranmore Hall* sports an 82B St Phillip's Marsh shedplate, so it's fair to assume that she has just brought a train into Paignton from Bristol for the seaside. However, you really should not assume – I assumed steam would last for ever, and how wrong was I! (28 August 1963)

Below right: Here's No 5992 *Horton Hall* again, pulling into Paignton. Wherever I went during that week on the Riviera she would be there. It probably meant that she was a favourite of the crews and reliable – perhaps as described by Marvin Gaye's record that was being played around this time, *Pride and Joy*. (28 August 1963)

Below: Taken from Skew Bridge, 'Hymek' No D7054 with a freight from the Plymouth direction passes the longer of the two platforms at Teignmouth (westbound), which was extended in 1938 to accommodate 15-coach trains, but is now long gone; conversely, the car park top right is still functional. (26 August 1963)

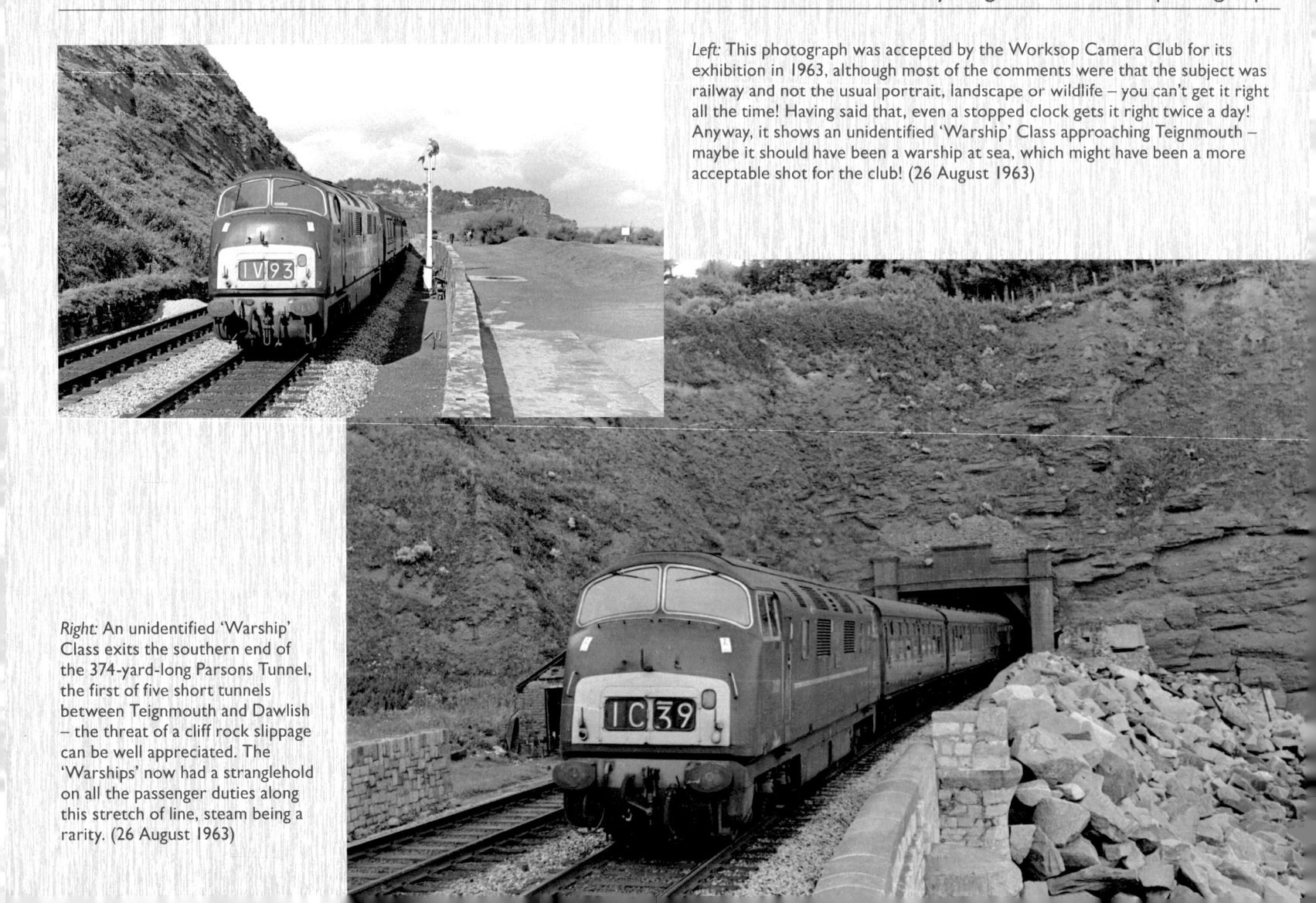

Left: This photograph was accepted by the Worksop Camera Club for its exhibition in 1963, although most of the comments were that the subject was railway and not the usual portrait, landscape or wildlife – you can't get it right all the time! Having said that, even a stopped clock gets it right twice a day! Anyway, it shows an unidentified 'Warship' Class approaching Teignmouth – maybe it should have been a warship at sea, which might have been a more acceptable shot for the club! (26 August 1963)

Right: An unidentified 'Warship' Class exits the southern end of the 374-yard-long Parsons Tunnel, the first of five short tunnels between Teignmouth and Dawlish – the threat of a cliff rock slippage can be well appreciated. The 'Warships' now had a stranglehold on all the passenger duties along this stretch of line, steam being a rarity. (26 August 1963)

Above: Hermes was a Royal Navy aircraft carrier that was unfortunately sunk on 9 April 1942 after being attacked by many Japanese dive-bombers as she headed for the Maldives, but here we have *Hermes* in the guise of 'Warship' Class No D823, and this is probably the nearest she will get to the sea. Strolling in the opposite direction is what looks like the local church minister and his curate heading towards Teignmouth. (26 August 1963)

Right: Here's a steam working rarity in the shape of Cardiff East Dock-based Class 9F 2-10-0 No 92219, only three years old and numbered one below the last-built No 92220 *Evening Star*, with a short goods train that is well within its capabilities. It is passing an interested group with the lady wanting a closer look than the others – or is she just taking a rest on the Dawlish seawall? (26 August 1963)

Above: Slowly passing through Dawlish station, which is literally on the beach, is 'Hall' Class No 4904 *Binnegar Hall* with one of the crew giving me the usual wave to a photographer. Unusually the platform edge was concrete but the rest of the construction was timber, together with all the fencing. (26 August 1963)

Above right: At nearly the same position an unidentified 'Warship' Class enters Dawlish station heading towards Plymouth and Penzance, as confirmed by the 'C' in the headcode. (26 August 1963)

Right: Another unidentified 'Warship', probably with a train from Plymouth, runs along the seafront approaching Dawlish station, with the Wall's ice cream litter bin on the right prompting you to 'PLEASE PUT YOUR WRAPPERS HERE'. On the left the menfolk of the time in formal attire are just ambling along the beach – it was quite normal to wear a suit in those days. With the exception of the suits and the litter bin this scene could be recreated today – everything is virtually the same. (26 August 1963)

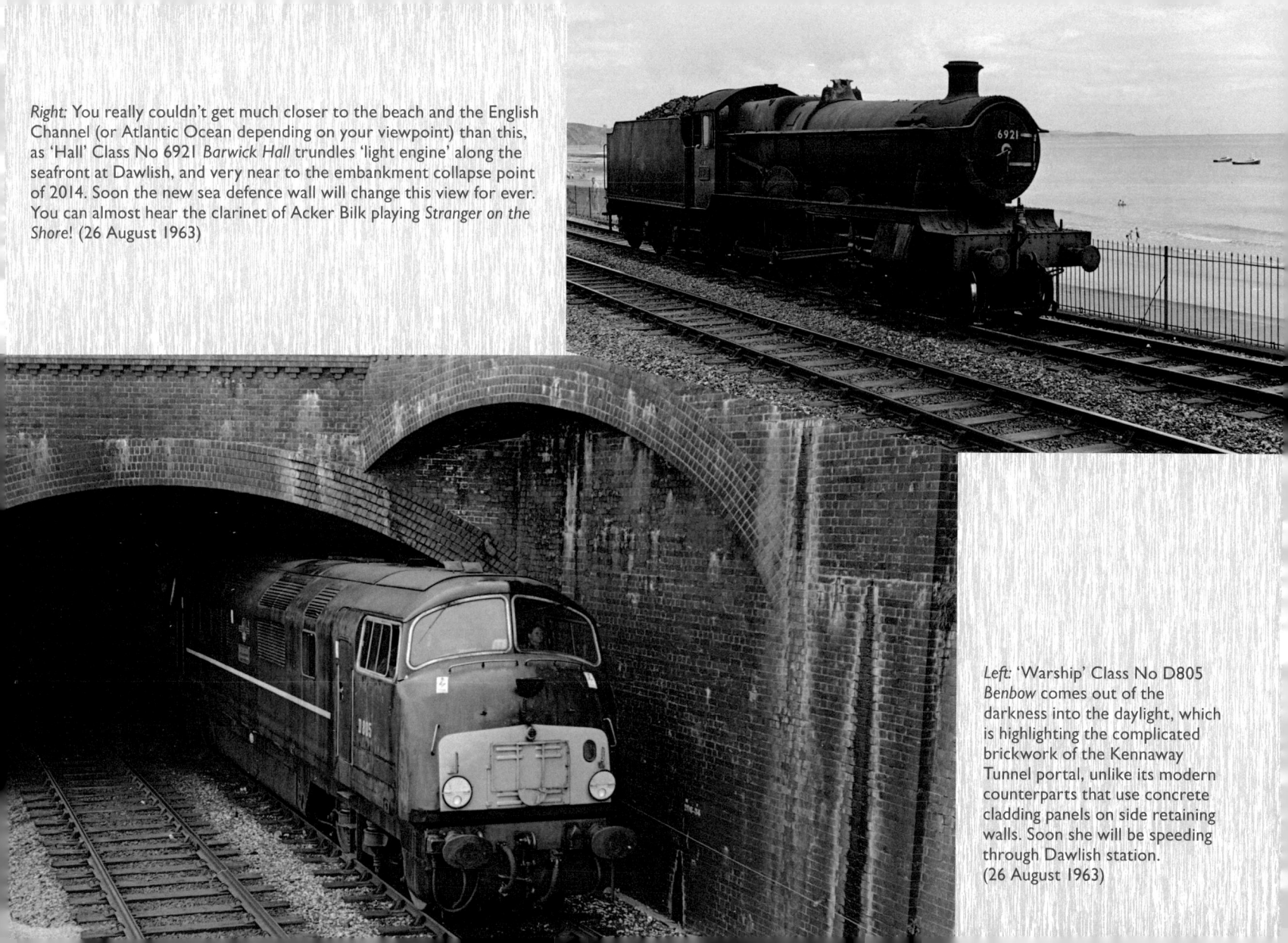

Right: You really couldn't get much closer to the beach and the English Channel (or Atlantic Ocean depending on your viewpoint) than this, as 'Hall' Class No 6921 *Barwick Hall* trundles 'light engine' along the seafront at Dawlish, and very near to the embankment collapse point of 2014. Soon the new sea defence wall will change this view for ever. You can almost hear the clarinet of Acker Bilk playing *Stranger on the Shore*! (26 August 1963)

Left: 'Warship' Class No D805 *Benbow* comes out of the darkness into the daylight, which is highlighting the complicated brickwork of the Kennaway Tunnel portal, unlike its modern counterparts that use concrete cladding panels on side retaining walls. Soon she will be speeding through Dawlish station.
(26 August 1963)

The long timber down platform at Dawlish station was devoid of any normal station infrastructure – nothing except the footbridge – with an old water tower and 'Warship' Class No D863 *Warrior* the only real points of interest. Nat King Cole was aptly singing about *Those Lazy, Hazy, Crazy Days of Summer*, and from memory that was really appropriate to the 'Riviera' back in August 1963. (26 August 1963)

The English Riviera

Left: One of the original batch of Warships, No D821 *Greyhound*, travels 'light engine' through Dawlish towards Newton Abbot. Without any yellow visibility panel, she resembles more the features of the derivative design from the German Krauss-Maffei V200 locomotive. (26 August 1963)

Right: 'Warship' Class No D843 *Sharpshooter* snakes round the nearly 2-mile coastal route bounded by the cliffs and the seawall between Dawlish and Teignmouth, which provides a good coastal walk and many photo opportunities. (26 August 1963)

2 • Barry and Woodhams

Ynys y Barri – Barry Island – was another seaside resort area mainly for day-trippers, but this time in Wales, and I was not on holiday but on an overnight Derbyshire Railway Society trip to the sheds with my mates Channy and Stuart Taylor. Going into Wales was a first for all of us, and the usual cracks about 'Will we need a passport?' and 'Will we ever get out?' were being bandied about in the coach.

Although a seaside resort, tourism was not the main industry; at Barry in the early 1900s it was the export of coal. According to records, in 1909 there were 8,000 women and 10,000 men employed in the docks, and by 1913 it was the busiest coal port in the world, exporting just over 11 million tons, surpassing Cardiff. However, the industry declined over the next 50 years and the importation of bananas from the Caribbean was established through the Geest company; although not approaching the monetary revenue of coal, it did provide some employment. In railway terms Barry is especially known for Dai Woodham and his scrapyard, but for us visiting in 1964 it was then just a scrapyard, and what was to evolve in future years couldn't have been imagined. Another trainspotting mate of mine was Michael Farmer; he had already been to Barry on holiday and he told me that from the station, although in the distance, you could see two 'Kings' in a scrapyard, and I should look out for them. Well, we didn't see them from a distance – we saw them close up, as can be seen from the following collection of photos at Woodhams in the early days.

Right: Class '5600' No 5637, one of Barry's own, is in the middle road on shunting duties, but in typical bunker-first mode; the trailing wheels helped negotiate the curves better, as these locos had a tendency to derail if going boiler-first. (June 1964)

Below right: 'Western' Class No D1039 *Western King* enters Barry station from the Cardiff direction. This could well have been one of the many seaside specials that ran at summer weekends. It is recorded that it was commonplace for the station to handle 30,000 passengers on summer Sundays; on Bank Holiday Monday in August 1957, 31 trains left Barry Island station between 5.00pm and 8.00pm, having arrived earlier in the day from the Midlands and the London area. (June 1964)

Barry and Woodhams

Right: Collett 'Grange' Class No 6867 *Peterston Grange* prepares to depart from Barry with a local service to Cardiff, this being one of her last duties as she was withdrawn on 31 August 1964. (June 1964)

Below: An analogy with Hemingway's *The Old Man and the Sea*, where for days the old man chased and wrestled with a fish (a marlin) only to see it get eaten by sharks, here we have an old man and his loco, and for days he's been coupling and shunting wagons with his Class '9400' No 8446 that was eventually eaten by the sharks at Birds scrapyard at Morriston on 30 November 1964. But before that she is seen stationary with the driver sitting comfortably, arms crossed and taking the heat of the cab and the outside sunshine in his stride. On the back of the pannier tank is a fireman's shovel and what may be a clinker tool/poker neatly stowed away. (June 1964)

Originally built in 1926 to a Class '5205' design, then rebuilt in 1934 to Class '7200', these 2-8-2Ts were the largest tank engines that ran on the Great Western. Here we see No 7208 standing in the yard at Barry sheds, already withdrawn in April 1964 and still reasonably intact but soon to be cut up at Birds of Risca in October. (June 1964)

In the brick-built six-road straight-through shed at Barry just a few locos are in residence and out of work for the weekend, but will be back to it on Monday. At the forefront in her home shed is Collett Class '5600' No 6648, built in 1928 for power and not speed, as the main duties these loco were employed on were short trips from the mines to the ports. (June 1964)

Right: Dai Woodham's yard is here in its infancy; preservation was not at the forefront of people's minds, but gathered momentum a few years later. Here are three views of the yard, with most of the locomotives intact and in reasonable condition. The above-ground hydrocarbon storage tanks are clearly visible; this facility had been built on reclaimed land that was once the West Pond site of Barry Dock. (June 1964)

Below: With Esso's marketing campaign 'I've got a tiger in my tank' in full swing during the 1960s, you might wonder if it would have done any good for all these tanks at Barry, to put some life back into them! These early views show all Western Region engines. Unfortunately some of the early arrivals did not make preservation, and were cut up; it was not until 1965 that stock from other regions started to arrive in numbers and all the empty rows became full, making photography very difficult in the cramped conditions. (June 1964)

Barry and Woodhams

Left: Another row of locos and a line of spotters nearly all wearing 'high-visibility' white shirts on this very hot day – how smart we were in those days! On the right are two of the old coal hoists that were used to transfer the coal from the rail wagons to the waiting boats at the dockside. In the heyday of coal-mining and movement there were dozens of hoists all around the perimeter of the docks. (June 1964)

Above right: On the cutting sidings in the West Pond area is one of the six ex-War Department saddle tanks that arrived at Woodhams during the summer of 1963, all by road and all scrapped by March 1965. Unfortunately, while my childhood spotting notes are mostly intact, the records for this trip to South Wales were lost. However, according to Peter Brabham in his book *Barry: The History of the Yard and Its Locomotives*, the numbers were 108, 178 and 203 from the Longmoor Military Railway, and the other three Nos 106, 119 and 130. (June 1964)

Left: One of three that sported Longmoor Military Railway (LMR) identification was Hunslet Engine Company 0-6-0 saddle tank No 203. By 1947 the War Department had a fleet of 377 of these saddle tanks, but as the war ended the fleet was reduced. Ninety were kept by the military, 75 were sold to the LNER and classified as 'J94', and 38 were loaned to the Dutch Railways; others were sold for industrial use. (June 1964)

One young lad's later trainspotting trips

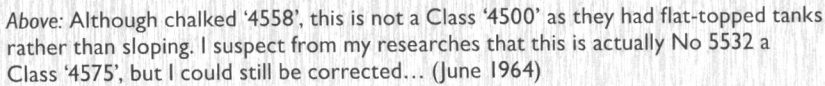

Above: Although chalked '4558', this is not a Class '4500' as they had flat-topped tanks rather than sloping. I suspect from my researches that this is actually No 5532 a Class '4575', but I could still be corrected… (June 1964)

Above right: This is one of the earlier designs, a Class '4500' with a flat-topped tank, but unidentified. (June 1964)

Right: Class '5205' No 5239 is in the Top Yard, hemmed in by Nos 5199 and 2874. The roof of the Barry Railway workshops can be seen in the background. (June 1964)

Left: This is an unidentified Class '2800'. Most of the tender engines did not have their tenders, which had likely been sold to the steelworks and used to transport ingots; another use for them was as sludge carriers. (June 1964)

Left: With 'Last of the Mohicans' chalked on the piston casing and minus her tender, 'Castle' Class No 5080 *Defiant*, true to her name, defied all intentions to convert her to scrap, finally ending up at Tyseley Locomotive Works after spending time on static display at the Buckinghamshire Railway Centre. (June 1964)

Above: This was my first sighting and experience of a 'King' Class, and for a 4-6-0, yes, they were big and impressive. Here is No 6024 *King Edward I* and, although she has been languishing since December 1962, she looks in reasonable condition externally, but was to spend 22 years idle at 'Woodhams by the Sea'. (June 1964)

Above right: No 6023 *King Edward II* arrived at Barry at the same time as No 6024 through fate, as both of the 'Kings' had been coupled together to perform a weight test on a bridge west of Bristol towards South Wales. Consequently after the test, with the pair now closer to Wales than Swindon, it was decided to sell them as scrap to Woodhams. It was fortuitous really – if they had gone back to Swindon they would now be in 'the railway in the sky'. What a stroke of luck! No 6023 was originally purchased as a spares donor for No 6024, but after years of restoration by various parties she has now morphed into a 'Blue King' at Didcot Railway Centre. (June 1964)

Right: The vast majority of the locomotives at Barry had none of the usual identification numbers on the smokebox or cabside; some had small stencilled numbers, some were chalked, but mostly you had to rely on the number stamped on the connecting rods for confirmation. Here we have 'Hall' Class No 4953 *Pitchford Hall*, but without connecting rods, so her identification must have been somewhere else. (June 1964)

Barry and Woodhams

Class 7F No 53808 had arrived only the week before, after being in service for years on the Somerset & Dorset line, and now dumped in the Top Yard at Woodhams. This was the first and the only one of the class I ever saw, although her sister No 53809 awaits me as she has been preserved. (June 1964)

This unidentified Class '5205', lying in Woodhams yard, would eventually go down in the history of Barry, but another event some 43 years later would also give fame to Barry. This was in the form of the comedy written by James Corden and Ruth Jones, *Gavin and Stacey*; if you look at the houses on the right by the wooden hoardings, Trinity Street is just out of the picture, with No 47 being the home of Stacey and family 300 yards up the hill. (June 1964)

3 • Severn Tunnel Junction, Newport and Cardiff

In the surrounding areas of Newport and Cardiff the coal industry was declining and industry was now predominantly steel. Richard Thomas & Baldwins Ltd opened in Newport in 1962 with 'jobs aplenty', and Cardiff had the well-established East Moors steelworks. The traditional employers in both Newport and Cardiff – the docks – were well into decline, exponentially tracking the mining industry.

This area and the nearby valleys are Wales's Rugby Union territory, with topics of conversation eventually coming around to the national sport. Coming second best was football, with rivalry between Newport and Cardiff. However, over the subsequent years the gap has widened, with Cardiff achieving Premiership status for a short while and Newport going out of existence, but being reborn in 1989 after taking on the Football Association of Wales at London's High Court and successfully winning their restraint of trade case – a wonderful example of 'little man beats big man'.

The South Wales area was a first-time visit for all three of us, so nearly everything we saw was a 'cop', albeit that the vast majority of sightings were locos stored and awaiting scrapping at the many Welsh scrapyards. The likes of Cashmore's at Newport were high in the league table of numbers scrapped at a location; again, it was early days at Cashmore's, and the famous scrap pile of locomotive parts was something for the future.

As a lad of 16 I could never have imagined that in another two years I would move to Newport and still be there some 54 years later, having married local girl Chris and worked there for 50 years, and now retired.

This is the view from the western end of the brick-built, six-road, straight-through shed at Severn Tunnel Junction, which had an allocation of around 70 steam locomotives. There is early evidence outside of diesels and what was eventually to come for the area – the shed closed for steam in 1965, totally closing in 1987. The marshalling yards at Severn Tunnel Junction were the largest in Wales with around 80 freight arrivals every day; the yards' original purpose was to sort the coal trains from South Wales for onward shipment to London and the Midlands, and to sort the good trains from the rest of the UK into Wales. The culverted watercourse on the right does not look too healthy, but then 56 years ago was that a priority? (June 1964)

From 1924 cars were transported by rail through the Severn Tunnel from Pilning as an alternative service to the Aust Ferry or the long road drive via Gloucester. Here we have two Class '5101s', Nos 4156 and 4132, coupled to a car transporter train loaded with Vauxhall Cresta, Hillman Minx, Mini and Austin A40 cars, then two covered up and a couple more. The rail service, together with the Aust Ferry, ended in 1966 with the opening of the first Severn Bridge. (June 1964)

Class '5101' No 4156 has uncoupled from the car transporter, revealing 'Love Boy' on the tank side – could that be him in the cab singing the Dean Martin song that was released the same month as the photo was taken, *Everybody Loves Somebody*. Members of Class '5101' were allocated to Severn Tunnel Junction primarily to perform piloting and banking duties through the Severn Tunnel to Patchway, but usually came off at Pilning. (June 1964)

Severn Tunnel Junction, Newport and Cardiff

An unidentified Class '2251' 0-6-0 with a mixed freight takes the line to Chepstow and Gloucester. The lines to Bristol and London, going through the nearly 4½-mile Severn Tunnel, are in the foreground, highlighted by the down gradient, eventually becoming 1 in 90, then roughly at the middle of the tunnel back up at 1 in 100. (June 1964)

From 2E Saltley, Class 9F No 92139 is resting after bringing a freight from the Midlands, which would have been uncoupled in the yards for sorting. She is seen at the eastern end of Severn Tunnel Junction shed, having already been turned on the turntable in preparation for the journey home. (June 1964)

Severn Tunnel Junction, Newport and Cardiff

Another visitor from the Midlands is Class 8F No 48459 from 2D Coventry. She will have to visit Severn Tunnel's turntable if she is to be rostered back north. It is evident by the encroaching weeds that the depot is in decline. (June 1964)

Outside Severn Tunnel Junction shed is a loco that has more than likely brought in a freight from the west, Class 9F No 92232 of Cardiff East Dock. She would be withdrawn some six months later after only six years of service and sent to Barry, to become one of a few that were regrettably scrapped by Woodhams. (June 1964)

Moving on to Newport, inside the roundhouse at Ebbw Junction are Class '4200' No 4214 accompanied by another unidentified Class '4200' (but with outside steam pipes) and Class '5700' No 4671. Some roundhouses were more conducive to photography than others due to good lighting, and Ebbw Junction was one of these – plenty of windows and whitewashed light-reflective walls that contrasted with the locomotives and all the metalwork of the shed. (June 1964)

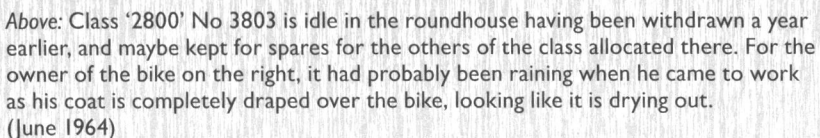

Above: Class '2800' No 3803 is idle in the roundhouse having been withdrawn a year earlier, and maybe kept for spares for the others of the class allocated there. For the owner of the bike on the right, it had probably been raining when he came to work as his coat is completely draped over the bike, looking like it is drying out. (June 1964)

Above right: 'Hall' Class No 5939 *Tangley Hall* has a lamp shade placed on the chimney and the piston refitting calculations chalked on the casing; both the end caps have still to be refitted. Parked next to the 'Hall' in Ebbw Junction is numerically the first 'Grange', No 6800 *Arlington Grange*; according to the Shangri-Las' pop hit of the year, it was the *Leader of the Pack*. (June 1964)

Right: 'Grange' Class No 6818 *Hardwick Grange* has obvious signs of leaks around the front end, which probably sealed her withdrawal notice that was served in April. She now stands at the west end of Ebbw Junction shed with a backdrop of houses on the Maes-glas estate, and awaits the 6-mile movement to Birds of Risca for scrapping. (June 1964)

Severn Tunnel Junction, Newport and Cardiff

Above: Also withdrawn and eventually cut up at Birds is Class '5205' No 5244. Our group of spotters are all wearing coats on to combat the early-morning cool at Ebbw Junction. The coaling stage is on the left and on the right is a watering point, with the Maes-glas road overbridge in the distance. The spotter with his back to the tank looks as though he is changing the film in his camera; this was always a pain if your 12 or 36 exposures had come to an end halfway round a shed, not like today when you just keep clicking, unlikely to fill the 128GB SD card! (June 1964)

Above right: Withdrawn in October 1963, numberplates and shedplate gone but both nameplates still intact, is 'Castle' Class No 5081 *Lockheed Hudson*. She was off 88B Cardiff East Dock and was withdrawn from there, so I am not sure why she was wasting away at Newport. According to records she was eventually scrapped at Birds in Bridgend at the end of June. (June 1964)

Right: Plenty of steam movement was evident in the yard at Ebbw Junction, with Class '4200' No 4233 joining in at the forefront of the scene, but withdrawn in October after 50 years of service. (June 1964)

Above left: Class '5700' No 3747 stands in the well-lit double roundhouse of Ebbw Junction alongside two six-plank trucks that were used for transporting the loco spares, although one is marked 'empty', a bit of useless information really! (June 1964)

Above: With the mounds of Maes-glas municipal waste tip visible in front of the boiler, Class '2800' No 2890 is wasting her time over the weekend at Ebbw Junction, but fortunately is still in service; that ended, however, in April 1965 and she was cut up at Birds of Risca in August. (June 1964)

Left: This looks like a line of withdrawn locos, but wrong – they were all still alive and undertaking various duties from the Newport shed, but maybe nothing for them on this weekend. First we have 'Castle' No 7034 *Ince Castle*, then 'Modified Hall' No 6992 *Arborfield Hall*, 9F No 92222 and 'Modified Hall' No 7910 *Hown Hall*. (June 1964)

Severn Tunnel Junction, Newport and Cardiff

Above: Class 9F No 92222 stands at Ebbw Junction, looking as though at one time it had an unofficial name on its 'blinker'. In one year's time she would be cut up about a mile from here at Cashmore's, Newport. (June 1964)

Above right: Withdrawn in September 1962 from 82B St Phillip's Marsh, and probably not having moved for nearly two years from this spot adjacent to the timber storage yards at Newport Docks, is Class '5101' No 4102. She was, however, soon to be cut up at Cashmore's just about half a mile down the tracks. (June 1964)

Right: In a long line of locos waiting for the torch at Cashmore's, Newport, is 'Castle' Class No 5097 *Sarum Castle*. During the 1960s more than 900 steam locomotives were cut up here, in round figures in excess of 90,000 tonnes of scrap. Virtually next door to Cashmore's was the private scrapyard of J. Buttigieg, which scrapped 130 locos, making Newport one of the largest graveyards for steam in the UK. (June 1964)

Below: Withdrawn two years earlier from Reading, but now close to where she takes her name from, St Fagans, Cardiff, home to the Welsh National Museum of History, is 'Castle' Class No 5067 *St Fagans Castle*, stored at the start of one of the scrap lines in Cashmore's. Withdrawn in July 1962, she was finally broken up here shortly after this photograph was taken, at the end of June 1964. The crane on the left of the picture was located in the area of the later infamous scrap pile. (June 1964)

Above: Having been withdrawn some 12 months earlier from Cardiff East Dock and doing her best to 'buck' the scrapping system is 'County' Class No 1001 *County of Bucks*. A Hawksworth design and built in 1945, during her nearly 24 years of service she had ten boilers fitted, and latterly had a double chimney. She lost the survival fight within the next few days and was cut up here at Cashmore's. (June 1964)

Severn Tunnel Junction, Newport and Cardiff

At Cashmore's, Newport, Class '4500' No 4567 looks a little worse for wear, but she had been withdrawn since 30 September 1962 and is seen standing just off the Octopus Bridge; two of the bridge's four sprigs ('tentacles') can be seen on the right and left. It was demolished in the 1990s when the whole area's road infrastructure was redeveloped, and a roundabout now occupies this spot, named Octopus Bridge Roundabout – the younger generation who were not around when the original brick bridge was there are somewhat bemused by the name! To the left, on top of the hill, is St Woolas Cathedral; for the granting of city status it was a prerequisite to have a cathedral – very fortunate for Newport! (June 1964)

Above: Adjacent to the factory buildings at Cashmore's, where they processed steel coils and turned them into sheets of various sizes and thicknesses for use by the steel fabricators located around South Wales, stands 'County' Class No 1004 *County of Somerset*. She awaits cutting up then smelting and remaking into coils for maybe Cashmore's to process – a different take on *Circle of Life* from *The Lion King* by Elton John and Tim Rice. At the right of the picture can be seen two of Cashmore's cranes that were located along the banks of the River Usk for offloading steel coils and assisting in the company's main scrapping 'arm', ships, hundreds of which were broken up here. (June 1964)

Above: Now we enter Cardiff East Dock shed, which was situated in the myriad of lines around the docklands, an area known as Tiger Bay. One of the approach roads to the shed was Bute Street, birthplace of the great Shirley Bassey. In the background can be seen many dock cranes, and to the right is the Pierhead Building of the old Bute Dock Company, and later of the Cardiff Railway Company. This magnificent red-brick construction still stands today and is the centre point of the completely redeveloped area known as Cardiff Bay. On the left, at the rear of the bunker of the Class '4200' – which I think is No 4242 – is a Hillman Imp and a Bond Minicar three-wheeler; as well as the locomotives, they are all desirable for preservationists! (June 1964)

Right: These Class '4200s' are 'chalked' Nos 4247 and 5231. You had to put your faith in the chalked numbers, with no reason to suspect that they were incorrect – a number was a number in those days! The main line to the right is now the dual carriageway that leads from Cardiff Prison to Cardiff Bay, and the shed yards are now the Red Dragon Centre, which houses a cinema, bowling, restaurants and Capital FM (South Wales) radio station. (June 1964)

Severn Tunnel Junction, Newport and Cardiff

Above: With the driver silhouetted in his cab, rather worse-for-wear Class 9F No 92236, an East Dock engine, trundles along the dead-end sidings road in front of a backdrop of the buildings and chimneys of East Moors Steelworks. All the tracks have now been lifted, and the area is now part of the dual-carriageway A4234 Central Link road accessing Cardiff Bay. (June 1964)

Above right: In the left background is Bute East Dock, with East Moors Steelworks on the right. Ironically, some of these locos after cutting up may have found their way back here to the smelting furnaces of East Moors. Here we see nearly 2,000 tonnes of potential scrap metal, at the forefront of which is Class '2800' No 2875. (June 1964)

Right: Rather clean Class '5205' No 5202 still bears an 88A (Cardiff Canton) shedplate, albeit that the shed had closed to steam in late 1962. Her home is now East Dock and she is parked just outside the main shed with the door open and inviting entry. (June 1964)

Withdrawn some six months earlier, 'Castle' Class No 5043 was built in 1936 and originally named *Barbury Castle*. However, in 1937 she was renamed *Earl of Mount Edgecumbe*, taking the name from No 3200, a member of the older 'Earl' Class. She was moved to Woodhams a few days after this shot, then after a nine-year stay by the seaside moved to Tyseley and is now part of that collection. (June 1964)

4 • Stockport and Bolton

Originally intended to be a chapter on the Manchester area, which was part of a week-long shed bash of the North West, North East and Scotland, it appears that a reel of 36 shots must have been lost some 50 years ago.

At the start of the day we visited Bolton and ended with Stockport Edgeley, with in between Agecroft, Newton Heath, Patricroft, Trafford Park, Longsight and Heaton Mersey. These six sheds produced 138 'cops' from 230 sightings, but no photographs. Only one sad conclusion – lost!

How things have changed in this area in respect of football. In Manchester, after United's domination for 50-plus years, they are now playing second fiddle to City, and at the moment it does not look as though there will be a re-emergence. Meanwhile Stockport has been from First Division to Conference North, and Bolton from Premiership to League One, with a 12-point deduction after going into administration. But whatever happens, fans are still loyal.

At Manchester Central Stanier Class 4 2-6-4T No 42462 has about another hour to wait before departure with the 8.30pm to Liverpool Central – a 45-minute service. This Manchester station closed in 1969 and became the GMEX Conference and Exhibition Centre, retaining all the features of the 64-metre single-span arch that was designed by Sir John Fowler. It was renamed Manchester Central in 2007 to rekindle the memories of the station. (31 July 1964)

Left: Class 4F No 44015 takes a break from shunting and repositioning the coaching stock in Gorton sidings, the driver contemplating his next move under the vast array of overhead wires that provided power on the Sheffield to Manchester 1.5kV DC line. (27 July 1963)

Below: At the eight-road dead-ended shed of Stockport Edgeley six locomotives are in steam outside and 12 more steaming inside. The shed survived nearly to the end of steam, closing in May 1968. Our group is just waiting for the permit exchange with the foreman to get the official nod to go round, but I was already on my way taking photos. (31 July 1964)

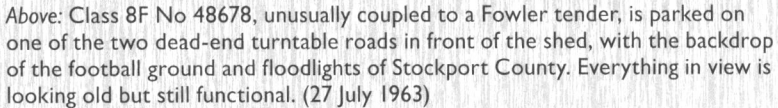

Above: Class 8F No 48678, unusually coupled to a Fowler tender, is parked on one of the two dead-end turntable roads in front of the shed, with the backdrop of the football ground and floodlights of Stockport County. Everything in view is looking old but still functional. (27 July 1963)

Above right: 'Jubilee' Class No 45632 *Tonga* is a long way from the 169-island archipelago in the Pacific, but relaxed at her home shed of Stockport Edgeley (9B). Built at Crewe in 1934, she completed nearly 31 years of service before being broken up at Cashmore's, Great Bridge. (31 July 1964)

Right: 1964 was the year that the Bahamas were granted internal autonomy and self-governing status by the British Parliament, but I don't think 'Jubilee' Class No 45596 *Bahamas* was particularly bothered about that as she simmered in Stockport Edgeley shed. Her status was that she was one of only three of the 'Jubilee' Class to have a double chimney, and is now preserved. It looks as though at one time she didn't have a 9B shedplate, just a 'painted-on' version. (31 July 1964)

One of the omnipresent 'WD' Class, No 90655 off 56D Mirfield, is reasonably clean at Edgeley, standing in front of Edgeley Park. On the right it looks like a good free football vantage point for railway workers on a Saturday afternoon! (31 July 1964)

Left: Who's making all the smoke – 'Jubilee' Class No 45596 *Bahamas* or the driver with a Woodbine? Never mind, smoking was considered fashionable and good for your wellbeing in those days, albeit that in 1962 a published report by the Royal College of Physicians – *Smoking and Health* – had quite the opposite findings. How times have changed! (31 July 1964)

Above: In Bolton shed is LMS Fowler Class 2F dock tank No 47164, introduced in 1928 and designed for work in docks, their short wheelbase allowing them to negotiate tight curves, aided by their Cartazzi self-centring axleboxes. There are not many stevedores here at Bolton, but for most of her life she was allocated to Birkenhead, the dockland Mecca of the North West. (31 July 1964)

Stockport and Bolton

Below: Indore in India originally had a metre-gauge railway, then at the beginning of the 21st century changed to a broad gauge of 5ft 6in, but our *Indore*, posing at Bolton as 'Jubilee' Class No 45592, is content with 4ft 8½in. She is viewed on the dead-end track in front of the shed building minus connecting rods and the centre pair of driving wheels, which were being serviced in the shed; quite a lot of interconnecting pipes with flanges are on the front buffer beam awaiting reassembly. (31 July 1964)

Above: Sheds in towns and cities were typically sited next to estates of terraced housing – OK if you were a trainspotter, but not a great selling feature if you weren't. Bolton shed commenced operations in the 1870s, and the housing could also have been late 19th century; the terraced design became popular, providing high-density accommodation for the working class. 'Crab' No 42708 didn't commence life until 1927. The shed closed 1968 and was demolished, and the 'Crab' was scrapped in September 1964, but from my research the housing is still providing dwellings at Bolton in Back Mayfield Avenue. (31 July 1964)

Left: A Patricroft engine, 'Black Five' No 44893 is all coaled up and the fireman appears to be carrying out his preliminary inspection and firebox preparation before the next duty out of Bolton shed. Originally a class of 842, encouragingly at this point in time there were still about 750 left. (31 July 1964)

Left: Standing next to the water pump at Bolton is Riddles BR 'Standard' Class 2MT No 84019, built at Crewe in 1953 and spending life on the London Midland Region except for a very short three-week spell at Eastleigh from 13 November 1965 until transferred back to the LMR on 6 December, only to be withdrawn on the 11th of that month. So latterly the Southern Region did not want her, and neither did the LMR! (31 July 1964)

Above: Outside Bolton Shed is one of 20 'Black Fives' to be fitted with Caprotti valve gear. No 44753 is seen from the front end, accentuating the original design modification; I suppose nowadays they might have had a gauging problem. It's a wonder the 'Thomas the Tank Engine' series hasn't adopted one, as the steam pipes would make great character arms to hug the Fat Controller! (31 July 1964)

Stockport and Bolton

Another of Bolton's five 'Crabs' was No 42705, simmering and looking all ready to pounce off the inspection pit and into action. However, the action lasted just a further five months – she was withdrawn on Boxing Day. (31 July 1964)

5 • The Glasgow area

With 1.2 million people living in the Greater Glasgow urban area in the 1960s, the city had its problems with a population density of 4,023 per square kilometre, high unemployment and urban decay, but rebuilding and regeneration projects had commenced. Clearing of the infamous slum areas like the Gorbals was under way and new high-rise flats were erected; however, this created more problems, social and health, due to the concentration of people in a small area. This resulted in another rethink some 30 years later, and the Queen Elizabeth Square flats were demolished to make way for a new housing development with a lower density, which it was hoped would improve the social aspect and safety in the area.

However, to spotters the area was a Mecca with four stations (Central, Queen Street, St Enoch and Buchanan Street) and nine sheds. We visited the area twice in November 1963 and July 1964, each time going round all the sheds. My records show that on our second trip, out of the 444 locos seen, 261 were 'cops', with a remarkable 133 locos on Polmadie, albeit that 43 were Clayton diesels! Here is a selection of photographs from both trips – the extreme weather conditions during each trip are very noticeable.

Above right: At the northern end of Eastfield shed is Class 'B1' No 61008 *Kudu* with another unidentified member of the class in front. There are sub-zero temperatures during an early-morning visit, and the shed yard lights are still lit. The viaduct carrying the Lanarkshire and Dunbartonshire section of the ex-Caledonian Railway, which was built to connect Balloch to Glasgow in the 1890s, can be seen elevated on the right. (30 November 1963)

Right: Posed on No 8 road of the 14-road straight-through shed at Eastfield is BR 'Standard' Class 4MT No 80004, introduced by Riddles in 1952. She was always a Scottish engine, based at Kittybrewster, Eastfield, Dawsholm and Corkerhill, then in 1962 spent 18 months at Beattock for banking duties on the arduous northward climb that culminated at 315 metres above sea level. (30 November 1963)

The Glasgow area

61

From Shakespeare's *Richard III*, 'Now is the winter of our discontent.' I can't agree with the discontent, as I was happy to be 'copping' all these foreign engines, but I can agree with the winter. Yes, it was cold, evidenced by the frost, particularly on the tender of Class 3F 0-6-0 No 57592. (30 November 1963)

Below: Little Johnny, having an English lesson at school, was asked by the teacher what was the collective noun for crabs? 'A dose, Miss!' Well, here is a dose of 'Crabs' at Eastfield, Nos 42752 and 42735 with 42736 at the rear. I think the dose they will get, though, is not crabs but flu in this sub-zero temperature. I know we were very cold that morning – was it to be a recurrence of the big freeze of the previous year? (30 November 1963)

Above: At the eastern side of Eastfield shed is the old manual coaling stage, which was made redundant in the 1930s when it was replaced by the mechanical coaling stage; apparently the old one was kept as a backup for a 'just in case' situation. In front of the dilapidated staging is Class 'A3' 'Pacific' No 60090 *Grand Parade*, some four weeks into her official withdrawal notice; this is difficult to understand as she was in Doncaster Works for 37 days from 10 July (my photograph of her there was included in the first book in this series on page 55), and was obviously outshopped in good running order, but two months later was condemned – must she have been surplus to requirements?
(30 November 1963)

The Glasgow area

Today spotters who took photographs in the 1960s reflect on how they wished they had had digital camera technology – but in this freezing weather just how long would the battery power have lasted? This 'V2' Class No 60822 did not last much longer, being withdrawn 12 months later after nearly 27 years of mixed-traffic work – and being used to the cold, as she was a Scottish engine all her life. (30 November 1963)

Above: In more favourable weather conditions, on a sunny summer's day at Eastfield 1938-built Stanier 2-6-4T No 42622, off Copley Hill, seems a long way from home for this type. She shares the roads with 'B1' No 61002 *Impala* and a 'Black Five'. In the words of the Grammy-winning folk hit written and performed by Gale Garnett and released in July 1964: 'We'll sing in the sunshine, We'll laugh every day, We'll sing in the sunshine, Then I'll be on my way.' (26 July 1964)

Above right: In a very grimy condition is 'Coronation' Class No 46228 *Duchess of Rutland*. You could just tell that it was maroon, but it was difficult to see the style of lining, which should have been LMS black and yellow. During her 26 years she was allocated to all the main sheds on the Midland Region – Camden, Crewe, Upperby, Holyhead, Edge Hill, Longsight and Rugby – but never to Polmadie, so she is here as a guest. In two months' time she would be guesting no longer! (26 July 1964)

Right: At Polmadie, with another two years to go before the inevitable, is 'Black Five' No 45195, with a lamp on the bracket positioned just below and to the right of the numberplate; a few of the class did have this bracket feature. (26 July 1964)

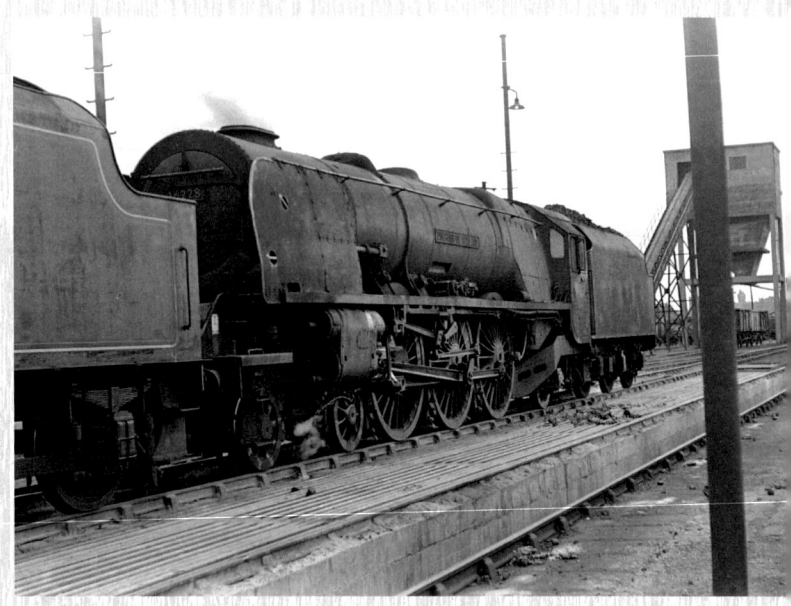

The Glasgow area

'Royal Scot' Class No 46115 *Scots Guardsman* is without its official crested nameplates and has been unofficially named *Everton FC*, a team that by default was caught up in the April 1964 British betting scandal, the main culprits being from Sheffield Wednesday – Peter Swan, David Layne and Tony Kay, who had been transferred to Everton in 1962 for a then British record of £60,000. The 'Scot' was off 12A Carlisle Kingmoor, and according to the train indication panel – 1S71 – has just brought in an express passenger service to Glasgow Central, and is now taking a rest in Polmadie. Fortunately she was preserved and is currently with the West Coast Railway Company, having just recently re-entered service after overhaul. (26 July 1964)

One young lad's later trainspotting trips

Above: Back in the winter, on her home shed of 66A Polmadie and with the light slowly breaking through the early-morning mist and smoke, nine-year-old BR 'Standard' Class 5MT No 73059 seems to be at full pressure and champing at the bit ready for the road ahead. (30 November 1963)

Above right: Back to 'brass monkey' weather, 'Royal Scot' Class No 46104 *Scottish Borderer*, after spending most of her life at Polmadie, has ended up on the scrap lines at Corkerhill, where she has lain dormant for the last year. (30 November 1963)

Right: With Darlington-style countersunk rivets on the cab and tender providing a smooth finish, this is Class 'A1' No 60131 *Osprey* off Neville Hill, probably having worked through from Leeds via the Settle & Carlisle line. Seen standing at Corkerhill, No 60131 was one of four 'A1s' to be given a bird's name that had previously been carried by an 'A4'. Her withdrawal came in October 1965, being sold to T. W. Ward of Killamarsh and cut up at that company's Beighton yard. (26 July 1964)

The Glasgow area

Above: Are the 'Scot' and my friend 'Channy' singing the much-recorded duet *Baby it's Cold Outside*? In his imitation suede coat – we were all jealous – 'Channy' enters the number in his notebook while walking away from 'Royal Scot' Class No 46102 *Black Watch*. A little bit more mist at Corkerhill and I would not have got a photograph; I don't think any adjustment to the aperture would have resulted in a better shot in those conditions, but then I was still learning by trial and error. (30 November 1963)

Above right: Out of the 48 locos on shed at St Rollox, 22 were diesels and 16 were 'Black Fives'. Here is one of them, No 44887 off Carlisle Kingmoor. Tucked away inside the shed, but with no chance of a photo, were two Class 'A4s', Nos 60027 *Merlin* and 60031 *Golden Plover*, both having been allocated there since early 1962 and performing on the 3-hour expresses from Glasgow Buchanan Street to Aberdeen; this was passionately known as the swansong of the 'A4s', but then all classes were singing their swansongs. (26 July 1964)

Right: Here at 65E Kipps, not the Hornby model 'Smokey Joe' but the real thing, a Drummond and McIntosh Caledonian saddle tank ('Pug') built in 1885. No 56029, withdrawn on 31 December 1962, finally went to Motherwell Machinery & Scrap for disposal in August 1964. (26 July 1964)

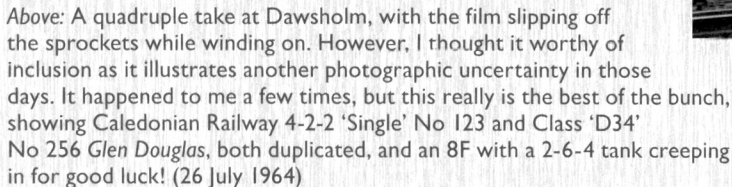

Above: A quadruple take at Dawsholm, with the film slipping off the sprockets while winding on. However, I thought it worthy of inclusion as it illustrates another photographic uncertainty in those days. It happened to me a few times, but this really is the best of the bunch, showing Caledonian Railway 4-2-2 'Single' No 123 and Class 'D34' No 256 *Glen Douglas*, both duplicated, and an 8F with a 2-6-4 tank creeping in for good luck! (26 July 1964)

Above right: Straits Settlements in South East Asia consisted of Malacca, Dinding, Penang and Singapore, and here we see them in Scotland as 'Jubilee' Class No 45629 *Straits Settlements* makes a spirited start heading south from Motherwell sidings adjacent to the sheds with a mixed freight. (30 November 1963)

Right: 'Black Five' No 45498 stands in Motherwell shed yard just in front of the ash and slag heaps that were eventually removed during the 1990s. However, there was cause for concern in 2011, and North Lanarkshire Council commissioned an investigation to check for residual radiological and chemical hazards to human health. In summary, the outcome was 'localised risk may exist' with recommendations for monitoring. Nothing conclusive then, but with a 'cover your backside' statement. (26 July 1964)

The Glasgow area

Leftt: 1963, the year of the Porsche 911, the Ford Corsair and the Toffee Crisp, also saw 'Black Five' No 45492 being affectionately cared for at Motherwell shed. Here you see one of the crew administering a little tender loving care. Behind is one of the unpopular Clayton diesels, No D8521 – she won't receive the same love, I'm sure. They were unreliable, with some of the class lasting less than five years before being scrapped. (30 November 1963)

Below left: With a stovepipe-style chimney, seen at Motherwell is McIntosh Class 3F No 56336, introduced in 1910 and withdrawn a year earlier, finally being scrapped in December 1963 after 52 years of service – nearly as much as *Dr Who*, first broadcast on 23 November 1963 and still with a loyal band of fans after 57 years, something that could go on for ever. However, the first programme started 80 seconds later than the scheduled time because of the assassination of President Kennedy the previous day. But being late did not worry William Hartnell – he was a 'Time Lord'… (30 November 1963)

Below: Withdrawn the day before this photograph was taken, Class 3F No 57681 is in the yard at Motherwell. Was the wooden wagon in the background specially made in advance for transporting loads of Microsoft software, having 'XP' painted on the side? (30 November 1963)

This was my only shot of a Type 1 Clayton. No D8518 is seen at Motherwell, and the photo, like the class, is not the best. The Claytons were introduced in 1962, with scrapping commencing in 1968. Loosely, one of the class featured in an episode of 'Thomas the Tank Engine' as 'Derek', and the episode was called 'Double Teething Troubles'. Need I say more? (30 November 1963)

6 • The North East

This was traditionally a depressed area after the decline of its main employers, mining, steel and shipbuilding, all of which had a 'knock-on effect on the railways. The movement by rail of raw materials and finished goods was getting less and depot allocations were reduced, not to be replaced one-for-one with the new diesels. The depression transferred itself through to the railway sheds; with the exception of Heaton, most were falling into disrepair, as is evident from my selection of photographs. For me, looking back now on 1963-64, the North East, together with South Wales, really gave the impression that the end was close for steam, with the unkempt locos and sheds and the lines of withdrawn engines. However, as I have stated before, at the time I was oblivious to all this, just a young lad taking numbers and photographs.

From memory, for whatever reason Gateshead did not issue permits for visits at around this time, which is a pity because, unlike the southern end of the former LNER, 'Pacifics' were still operating regularly in the North East. According to Paul Bolger in his *BR Steam Motive Power Depots: NER*, in 1959 39 'Pacifics' were allocated to Gateshead, more than were allocated to King's Cross Top Shed at that time, so we were disappointed not to be visiting. However, today records reveal that at the time of our North East visit the depot only had an allocation of 18 steam locomotives in total, so really not much was missed.

Dilapidated is an understatement to describe the roundhouses of Tyne Dock – lack of roofing, crumbling brickwork, broken windows and generally unkempt. Class 'Q6' No 63431 stands on one of the roads among ash-covered tracks with the lifting gear appearing to be the only thing that has had any sort of upkeep from the shed staff. (27 July 1964)

Above: This part of the Tyne Dock roundhouse buildings did have about 6 metres of roof left, just about as far as the smoke extractor over Class 'J72' No 68704, who has her sister No 69025 on the left. Both of them are out of service and with ragged chimneys. (27 July 1964)

Above right: In the yard at Tyne Dock these two Class 9Fs were still employed. Nos 92061 and 92066 are both fitted with Westinghouse air pumps for the workings to Consett; there were 14 trains daily, each with a rake of nine 56-tonne-capacity dual-compartment ore wagons that had air-operated doors – two on each side of the wagon – to enable rapid unloading of the ore. (27 July 1964)

Right: With its tender just under the arched entry point to the westerly roundhouse of Tyne Dock, Class 'Q6' No 63411 stands alongside No 63360, both in steam and each having two indication lamps on their front ends, at the ready. (27 July 1964)

The North East

Above left: Shed bashes were becoming more and more like scrap-line bashes. Here at 52B Heaton in the dump are two Class 'J72s', Nos 69008 and 69016, both with their numbers painted on the tank side, Darlington-style. Behind them are Class 'V2' No 60964 and Class 'A3' No 60070 *Gladiateur*, with a lot more out of the picture. (27 July 1964)

Above: Further along the lines at Heaton is Class 'V2' No 60904 with separate cylinder castings, a modification from the monobloc system made during a 38-day General Overhaul at Darlington in 1957. Having been withdrawn from Gateshead shed some 18 days earlier, in August she was sent from Darlington Works to Swindon Works for breaking up – the economics of that are hard to comprehend! (27 July 1964)

Left: Another sorry sight at Heaton is Class 'A4' No 60002 *Sir Murrough Wilson*. Having always sported a corridor tender and allocated to Gateshead for her entire life, she is pictured on the scrap line at Heaton with no nameplates or dome, idle and just waiting to be cut up, which was soon to take place at Cohen's, Cargo Fleet. Gateshead did not have a reputation for clean locos, so if she was in service you would not have noticed much of a difference, except that she would have had a nameplate and a dome. (27 July 1964)

For some of us it was 'Manna from Heaven', not in the form of food for the Israelites but a 'cop' for trainspotters – Class 'A3' No 60085 *Manna*. Inside Heaton's eight-track straight shed all the engines were in very clean condition. Officially the shed had closed in June 1963 but was subsequently used for storage and stabling. (27 July 1964)

The North East

Above left: Credit must go to the management of Heaton for adopting a 'keep it clean' policy – everything in the photograph is spotless, perhaps the cleanest steam depot I visited. Here we have a couple of Gresley Class 'V3' 2-6-2 tanks, Nos 67646 with 67636, and Sulzer Type 4 No D128 poking her nose in. (27 July 1964)

Above: At Heaton and still with a 52B shedplate but actually allocated to 52A is 'highwayman' *Dick Turpin*, Class 'A3' No 60080. It is in what I consider to have been their best appearance: Brunswick Green, double chimney, German-type smoke deflectors and Great Northern-style tender. The real Dick Turpin met his end at York, hanged in 1739, but this one met its end cut up at Draper's yard, Hull, in December 1964. (27 July 1964)

Left: Designed by Wilson Worsdell and introduced in 1906, Class 'J27' No 65828 poses in North Blyth shed with a backdrop of houses on a road named, I presume, in his honour, Worsdell Street. Nineteen engines were on the shed, and I 'copped' the lot. (27 July 1964)

76 — One young lad's later trainspotting trips

Another Class 'J27', No 65845, poses in steam next to the ramp for the coaling stage at North Blyth, with her tender having been fully loaded for duty. Built in 1908 and withdrawn in 1965, how many tons of coal had she hauled? (27 July 1964)

The North East

Above left: From North Blyth shed it was about half a mile as the crow flies but 4 miles by road to navigate over the River Blyth and into South Blyth shed, and two more of my favourite 0-6-0 tender engines, Class 'J27' Nos 65882 and 65838. (27 July 1964)

Above: All of Gresley's 'V1' and 'V3' Classes were based in the North East and Scotland from their build date commencing in 1930. Here doing a bit of shunting work along the main line adjacent to South Blyth shed, just visible on the left, is Class 'V3' No 67638, which would be withdrawn four months later. There were only 12 on shed, but again all 'cops'! (27 July 1964)

Left: Seen from a road overbridge and with very little time really to compose the shot, or it would have been lost, is Class 'J27' No 65814 going tender-first with a loaded train into the Consett Steelworks, and passing the sheds, which are on the left out of view. (27 July 1964)

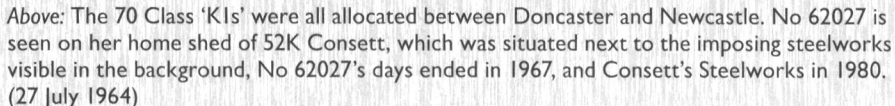

Above: The 70 Class 'K1s' were all allocated between Doncaster and Newcastle. No 62027 is seen on her home shed of 52K Consett, which was situated next to the imposing steelworks visible in the background, No 62027's days ended in 1967, and Consett's Steelworks in 1980. (27 July 1964)

Above right: Consett was a very small two-road shed with yards that had limited space, causing problems for the loco allocation and any visitors. Simmering outside on home territory are two Class 'Q6s', Nos 63427 and 63357. (27 July 1964)

Right: At the northern end of Consett shed on the dead-end track that could only be accessed by going through the shed is Class 'Q6' No 63394, at home but sporting the 52C shedplate of Blaydon – she had been transferred from Blaydon a year earlier! One shed door is closed, so had she been trapped in that spot since then, and was British Railways adopting the Swinging Blue Jeans' current hit, *You're No Good*? (27 July 1964)

Moving on to Sunderland, we see one of the ubiquitous North East Class 'J27s' in the form of No 65885, not getting much attention from the three spotters, who have found something a lot more interesting. (27 July 1964)

At home at Sunderland is Class 'Q6' No 63458, but with the pre-1948 British Railways number format on the side – LNER No 3458 – a nice touch by somebody. Maybe one of the old school is the guilty party! (27 July 1964)

The North East

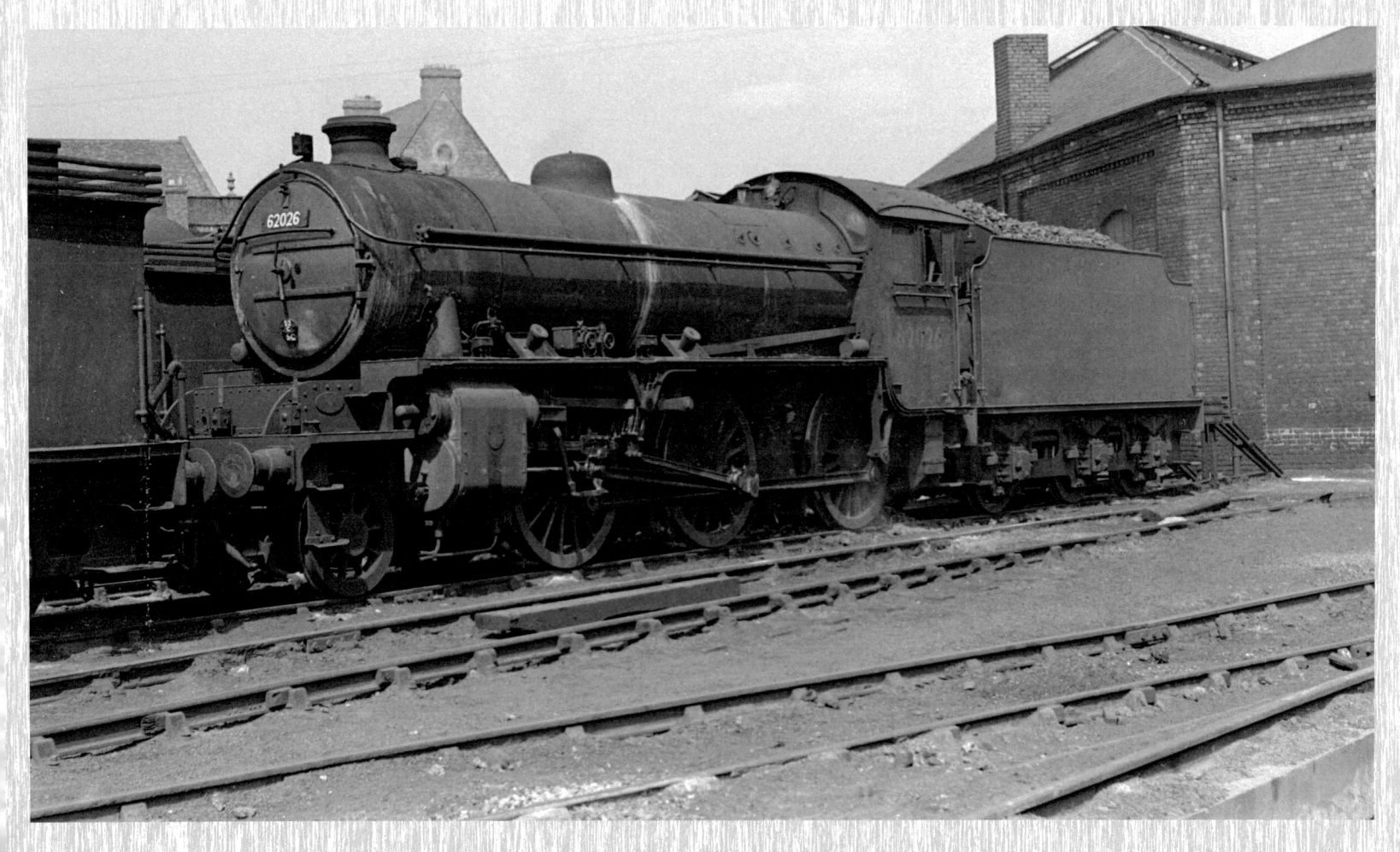

Outside in the yard at Sunderland with a leaky dome is Class 'K1' No 62026, backed up against the wall of the roundhouse with the entry tracks at the bottom right converging into one road with an inspection pit. (27 July 1964)

One young lad's later trainspotting trips

Left: In addition to the roundhouse at Sunderland there was a four-track dead-ended straight shed, and outside is Class 'Q6' No 63387 from Blaydon Races territory, 52C. Just inside the shed is an 'antelope' in the form of Class B1 No 61035 *Pronghorn*. Although murky around the shed, the sun was out, and it really was out two months later on 15 September for the launch of the *Sun* newspaper, which now has the largest circulation of any daily in the UK. With centre to right-wing principles, it is amazing how many Labour voters read it – don't they know, or are they just looking at Page 3?
(27 July 1964)

Right: In the roundhouse at Sunderland we have three Class 'J27' perennials demonstrating their 'planting' tolerances – Nos 65853, 65832 and 65873 are in shade, partial sun and full sun respectively! The lines that radiate from the turntable seem purposely designed to accommodate the 0-6-0 tender engines – anything longer has 'had it'! (27 July 1964)

7 • The Swansea area

In the 19th century Swansea (Abertawe) was the market leader in copper smelting, with the ore coming from all over the world for processing, and earning the area the name 'Copperopolis'. However, towards the end of the century the price of copper dropped considerably, thus making the transportation of the ore to Swansea unviable. With this demise and the decline of other heavy industries, the area had to reinvent itself and now the main employers are in the service sectors, notable examples being DVLA, BT and Virgin Atlantic.

Probably the most notable person from Swansea was the poet and writer Dylan Thomas (1914-53), who during his short life produced many literary masterpieces. One of his works, *Under Milk Wood*, was eventually made into a film, the cast including Richard Burton, Elizabeth Taylor, Peter O'Toole, Glynis Johns, Victor Spinetti, Ruth Madoc and David Jason – what an 'A' list!

Neath is on the original rail system developed by the Rhondda & Swansea Bay Railway at the turn of the 19th century, but from the outset it was never financially viable and in 1906 the Great Western Railway took control. Forsaken outside the carriage & wagon repair shops on the left at 87A Court Sart shed is Class '4200' No 4252, withdrawn a year earlier and cut up at the end of the month at Hayes/Birds of Bridgend. (June 1964)

The main shed at Swansea was Landore, which closed as a steam shed in 1961 for redevelopment into a diesel depot, reopening in 1963. It evolved through the years to become the service depot for the GWR fleet of InterCity 125s, but closed again in 2018 after they were phased out to be replaced by the Class 800 units. With another reprieve in September 2019, it reopened as a rolling stock repair centre for Chrysalis Rail. Since 2005 it has shared the area – across the road – with Swansea City Football Club at their new ground, the Liberty Stadium.

At the side of piles of ash in Court Sart stands a row of Class '5700' pannier tanks. All had been withdrawn in May, and with the McCoys telling Sloopy to *Hang On*, they were all trying to take that advice, but eventually succumbed in August and were scrapped. No 3731 is 'chalked', but still had the cast plates! (June 1964)

In steam, and in the minority, as most of the locos on shed were dead, is Class '5700' No 9609, standing in front of the elevated track leading to the coaling stage. The whole structure has a visually pleasing stonework pattern, most unusual for a shed. Court Sart closed in June 1965 and No 9609 was transferred to Llanelly – as it was referred to in the Ian Allan shed books (Llanelli being the correct spelling and pronunciation) – but only for a short while, being withdrawn in October. (June 1964)

Withdrawn from Llanelli in May, but now standing on the lines at Court Sart and looking as though the demolition squad are about to drop the wrecking ball on her cab, is Class '5700' No 3761, a Swindon-built Collett pannier tank. (June 1964)

The Swansea area

This is one of ten photos from my collection where I cannot positively identify the location. However, I am fairly certain that this is either Llantrisant or Tondu (it would have been taken with the shed at the back of me), and we see English Electric Type 3 No D6635 on a mixed goods. Any confirmation of the location is welcome. (June 1964)

Built at Swindon in 1936, Class '5700' No 9778 stands at the northern end of Llantrisant shed. Upon the shed's closure later in October, she was transferred to Radyr, maybe thinking that it would present a new lease of life, but alas her 'shelf life' was up, and she was withdrawn in November. (June 1964)

The Swansea area

89

Standing outside the southern end of the three-road straight-through shed of Llantrisant, together with a young spotter, is Class '5700' No 3617. Inside is another pannier tank and what looks like a 2-8-0, both unidentified, but all having bunkers full of, I would think, local Welsh coal. (June 1964)

Serenity – the only movements are the shadows. Class '4200' No 4222 stands outside the third road of the shed. My observation on visiting sheds was that the smaller the shed, the more likely you were to see locomotives that were still in service; it was the larger sheds with more space and track availability where there were lines of locos awaiting scrapping. This opinion was borne out here at Llantrisant. (June 1964)

The Swansea area

Left: In a sidings off the main line at Tondu is Class '1400' No 1422. She had actually been withdrawn in June 1957, some seven years earlier, and looking back on my records the earliest *abc Combined Volume* I had was the Summer 1959 edition, and No 1422 was not listed, so here is a loco that I was never to underline although it was a 'cop'! I'm not sure how long she had resided at this spot, but looking at her you would think a long time. The chalking is interesting, listing three 'Black Fives', a 'King', a Class '1400', and 'DOLER', which is a Spanish verb meaning to hurt or to cause pain – whoever visited on 16 May 1964 will know! You will notice that the spotters are running – this was because we had been told to be quick getting the numbers in this remote siding. (June 1964)

Above: Although parked next to the 'lifer' Class '4200', No 4262 hasn't been there that long, after hauling many millions of tons on local coal trains since she was built in 1919. She was withdrawn in April 1964, so ever so slightly 'still warm'. (June 1964)

Below: Nicely illuminated in the yard at Landore is another of the Western Region's lightweight diesel-hydraulics; 'Hymek' No D7085 was allocated to Cardiff, so is not far from home, but staying over. (June 1964)

Above: In 1963 Bobby Vee sang *The Night Has a Thousand Eyes* – well, our coach party of 40 didn't have that many, but we were able to see inside the well-lit 87E Landore shed in the middle of the night. Inside the shed are two 'Westerns' and two English Electric Type 3s. (June 1964)

The Swansea area

Below: A mysterious phantasm of a group of spotters is seen at Landore in this time-lapse photo, which is focusing on an unidentified 'Western' – and that's another mystery! The old footbridge visible on the right giving access from Pentre Treharne Road crosses over the West Wales line; the bridge is still there today but with both ends blanked off. (June 1964)

Above: Inside the clean and well-lit Landore shed, which opened in 1963, is English Electric Type 3 No D6869 receiving some attention – but not at present as the fitters had gone home, since it was about 3 o'clock in the morning. Only idiots like us were up at that time! Having said that, I *was* an idiot when I woke up to find I had missed Aberbeeg and Aberdare sheds because I had fallen asleep on the coach! (June 1964)

8 • The Birmingham area

Birmingham is an area of the UK culinarily renowned for its Indian restaurants, more specifically balti in the 'Balti triangle' of restaurants situated on the roads of Ladypool Road, Stoney Lane and Stratford Road to the south of the city centre. The dish was invented in Birmingham in the 1970s, and to qualify as a balti the ingredients must include turmeric, fresh ginger, garam masala and fenugreek, all cooked in a pressed steel dish. In 2015 balti was given EU Protected Name Status, but as I write this I am unsure what will happen after Brexit – perhaps I should ask Boris?

The city is the second largest in the UK and at the time of my visit some of its traditional industries still survived, including Cadburys, the Austin, Land Rover and Jaguar car plants, and the many light engineering workshops. Probably the most famous car produced there was the Mini, introduced in 1959 and designed by Alec Issigonis at the Longbridge plant with its revolutionary transverse engine and front-wheel drive.

For me this trip was a first to the area and was a typical organised one-day shed bash with the Derbyshire Railway Society, visiting nine sheds. All we had to do was get to Derby from Worksop for the coach pick-up, then all the work was done for us, chauffeured to each shed!

In the roundhouse at Tyseley is '5700' Class pannier tank No 3770 in the company of 9F No 92215 and 'Castles' Nos 5014 *Goodrich Castle* and 7003 *Elmley Castle* with another 9F, No 92065, just outside the shed maybe waiting to make an entry into the roundhouse, as the turntable is correctly positioned. (5 July 1964)

Above: Class '4500' No 4555 is all spruced up at Tyseley with 'GREAT WESTERN' painted on the side tanks. She was eventually purchased by Patrick Whitehouse and Pat Garland for £750, which included a light overhaul. She now resides at the South Devon Railway, which was established as the Dart Valley Railway in 1965. (5 July 1964)

Above right: Three 'Castles' are all in steam at Tyseley: from left to right, they are Nos 5014 *Goodrich Castle*, 7003 *Elmley Castle* and 7013 *Bristol Castle*. Actually, *Bristol Castle* was in reality No 4082 *Windsor Castle*, the pair having exchanged identities in 1952. No 4082 had been allocated the duty of drawing the funeral train of King George VI from London to Windsor, but was being overhauled at Swindon at the time, whereas No 7013 had recently been outshopped from the works and was in first-class condition — hence the switch, which was never reversed. (5 July 1964)

Right: Although not withdrawn, but looking in a very sorry state at Tyseley, 'Hall' Class No 4929 *Goytrey Hall* appears to be 'dead', unsurprisingly! The stately home Goytrey Hall was built in 1446 close to Pontypool, but has undergone a change and is now a farmhouse; the spelling has also changed and is now Goytre. (5 July 1964)

Of quite a futuristic design was the Western Region six-car diesel-electric 'Blue Pullman' set, seen here partially inside No 2 road at Tyseley for the weekend, as the morning service between Wolverhampton Low Level and Paddington and the afternoon service from Birmingham Snow Hill to Paddington were scheduled on weekdays only. They were considered as luxury train services, aimed at the businessman of the 1960s, and I bet there were a few pin-striped suits and bowler hats on view, let alone a silk handkerchief in the top pocket! (5 July 1964)

The Birmingham area

Above: Just two days old after entering service from the Brush Traction Works at Loughborough on 3 July 1964, Brush Type 4 No D1747 stands in the yard at Tyseley awaiting acceptance trial runs on Monday, then going to 81A Old Oak Common for the next three years. (5 July 1964)

Above right: Saltley was a shed where you could get classes from all regions except the Southern on a regular basis, and here we have a Class 9F off Barrow Road, a Class 8F off Toton and a Class 'B1' off Canklow, Nos 92248, 48361 and 61167 respectively, all in steam. (5 July 1964)

Right: In the yard just in front of the three-roundhouse building at Saltley are two 'Hall' Class locos, Nos 6932 *Burwarton Hall* and, behind, 6942 *Eshton Hall*, withdrawn in December 1965 and December 1964 respectively. (5 July 1964)

Built at Derby, nine months old but not looking anything like newish from Northampton (2E), and boxed in at Saltley is Sulzer Type 2 No D7570. Twenty of the class survived into preservation, but not all are yet operational. (5 July 1964)

Above left: Class 8F No 48747 approaches Bescot yards with a freight. Part of the elevated section of the M6 motorway, still under construction, can be seen on the left framed by the footbridge. (5 July 1964)

Above: No 49361, a London & North Western Railway Class 'G2A', nicknamed 'Super D', is in steam at Bescot, but more than likely parked for the weekend. The class did not have much time left; this one was withdrawn in December 1964 and cut up locally at Cashmore's, Great Bridge, after 61 years of service. (5 July 1964)

Left: The front third of 1947-built Ivatt Class 4MT No 43002 looks in reasonable condition, but it gets visually worse as you move along the boiler. There were 54 locos on shed, and I 'copped' 44 – not bad! (5 July 1964)

A general view of the eight-track dead-ended shed at Nuneaton. It had an allocation of 40, and we saw 47 on shed, all in steam. I 'copped' 27. (5 July 1964)

The Birmingham area

Above: Half of Nuneaton's allocation were Class 8Fs, and here we have three, left to right Nos 48623, 48292 and 48686, two of which were on their home shed and the other, No 48692, was visiting from Speke, in the middle and probably unable to get a word in! (5 July 1964)

Above right: Pulling away from Nuneaton station with a rake of eight heading for Rugby and beyond, Sulzer Type 2 No D5030 passes under a myriad of overhead electrification gantries and wires, but no pantographs on her to conduct the electricity as she is a diesel. The electrics were her successors, just as the diesel had been successor to steam; progress is strange, quite often proving that the investment made was uneconomical and 'knee jerk'. (5 July 1964)

Right: In mathematical terms the train identification headboard has a somewhat large combination of digits and variables, '9Z28U8W', making it more like an algebraic expression – it seems a lot for a signalman to identify if the train was passing his box at 50-plus! You can't even read the smokebox numberplate, but it is 'Black Five' No 44715 parked outside Nuneaton shed. (5 July 1964)

One young lad's later trainspotting trips

Below: I must have been lying down when I took this picture of 'Castle' Class No 7011 *Banbury Castle* and Class 8F No 48094 at Oxley. It's quite OK, though, as they are both stationery at 2B – or not to be! (5 July 1964)

Right: For me 'Brits' always look better photographed from the rear, revealing all their complex pipework and the wheel arrangement, which is accentuated by the high running plate that was a deliberate design feature to ease maintenance. Here we have a reasonably clean example of the class, No 70020 *Mercury*, fired up just outside Nuneaton shed. (5 July 1964)

Above: Now we see a grimy 'Britannia Class', No 70015 *Apollo*, at Oxley with a lineman talking to one of the crew who is disregarding the build-up of steam pressure and just letting the safety valves take care of it. You can just see the front step modification that was introduced by Stratford shed in 1953/54 to allow the crews to reach the top lamp iron to locate the headboards; however, that fitted to *Apollo* looks like the later Crewe Works variant, which eventually outmoded the others. You can also see the Western Region-style brass-lined handholds on the smoke deflectors, six on each, the modification having been carried out at Swindon Works around 1957 just for the nine of the class that were based at Cardiff Canton. (5 July 1964)

Above right: In respect of the music genre, who put the 'c' in 'rap'? Well there is an assortment of 'rap' at Oxley in front of Class 5MT No 45283, but she did manage to last 30 years, not becoming in British Railways' eyes 'rap' until May 1967, then broken up by Cashmore's of Great Bridge. (5 July 1964)

Right: 'Castle' Class No 5000 *Launceston Castle* is in what was possibly her final parking spot, as she was officially withdrawn from Oxley in October. During her 38-year life she had a new boiler fitted roughly every two years (16 in total) and was paired with 33 different tenders. She is seen here with Diagram HC boiler No 7616 and Hawksworth tender No 4095 – but no smokebox numberplate! (5 July 1964)

Above: Hackness is a civil parish in North Yorkshire and according to the 2001 UK census had a population of 96, but the census of 2011 revealed a more than 100% increase to 225. No 6925 *Hackness Hall* appears to have been blessed with a 'sixth sense' and knows that the population there will soon be having a good time, so no wonder she has a smiley face at Oxley! (5 July 1964)

Above right: Still at Oxley, here's smart-looking 'Grange' Class No 6848 *Toddington Grange*, currently based at 85A Worcester and finally withdrawn from there in December 1965 after 28 years on the Western rails, being eventually cut up at Cashmore's, Newport, in April 1966. (5 July 1964)

Right: Also at Oxley is 'Manor' Class No 7827 *Lydham Manor*, technically not a Great Western engine but a British Railways one, having been built in 1950 and therefore a relatively young engine of 14 years. Still in steam and having a tender full of coal, with some really big lumps, she would go on for another 14 months before being sold to Woodhams at Barry; fortunately she only spent four years there before being purchased by the Dart Valley Railway. (5 July 1964)

The Birmingham area

A visitor to Oxley from Manningham is Fairburn Class 4MT 2-6-4 tank No 42093. Built at Brighton in 1951, she spent three years on Southern rails before moving to the North East, then Yorkshire. Two of the class have survived and are both on the Lakeside & Haverthwaite Railway. Fine-looking engines, I always called the 2-6-4s 'Pacifics in Reverse'! (5 July 1964)

One young lad's later trainspotting trips

Above: 'Grange' Class No 6866 *Morfa Grange* looks out on a limb in an overgrown siding at Stourbridge shed, although she is fully coaled and you can just detect a little smoke coming from the chimney, perhaps to the beat of the Hollies' hit *Here I Go Again*, so all is not lost! (5 July 1964)

Above right: Standing on one of the five tracks on the south-west side of Stourbridge shed is Kettering-based Class 8F No 48645, with a lamp bracket on the side of the smokebox door. Many 8F locomotives were built for the War Department and served in war-torn Middle East countries; a few did make it back to blighty, but others were not so lucky. (5 July 1964)

Right: A Welsh engine from Neath at Stourbridge, and due to be withdrawn in a month's time, is Class '2800' No 3860. With a few small hills in the background or maybe spoil heaps that have now been flattened, the area is now a large housing development, a far cry from this desolate-looking area. (5 July 1964)

Above: Another one all alone in Stourbridge is Class 9F No 92002 with no trailing wheels or coupling rods. However, they must have been somewhere under repair as she lasted another three years, operating from Tyseley, Saltley and Birkenhead, being finally withdrawn from Speke. (5 July 1964)

Above right: An operational resident of Stourbridge shed for the past 11 years is Class '5600' No 6683, simmering at the extent of the partial electrification within the shed yard. Did they run out of money, or what? (5 July 1964)

Right: Now inside the roundhouse at Stourbridge, with her smokebox door open for cleaning maybe, is Class '5101' No 4133, beside a slowly running water hydrant and with the shed body-building equipment just in front! (5 July 1964)

One young lad's later trainspotting trips

Above: 'Hall' Class No 5990 *Dorford Hall* is perfecting her balancing act on four wheels prior to an interview with Cirque du Soleil! From this photo it is noticeable how much larger the radiating tracks are in Stourbridge than the ones seen earlier at Sunderland. (5 July 1964)

Above right: Standing behind the pile of springs is Class '7400' pannier tank No 7432 at her home shed of Stourbridge. On this day in Turkey, Talat Aydemir, an Army Colonel, was hanged after two attempted coups d'état in 1962 and 1963 – but in Stourbridge I had a 'cops d'état' of 56 out of 64! (5 July 1964)

Right: In Stourbridge, with their age difference negligible, are BR 'Standard' Class 5MT No 73070, built in 1954, and 'Castle' Class No 7034 *Ince Castle*, built in 1950, both born in the years of nationalised British Railways. You tend to think that the 'Castles' were all old, with the originals having been introduced in 1923. (5 July 1964)

Class '5700' No 8718 stands just outside 2P Kidderminster shed. Made of corrugated-iron sheeting, and now looking the worse for wear, the shed was opened in 1932 to replace the original structure near the station. A two-road shed, in its heyday it had an allocation of 16; on my visit there were 11 on shed, all 'cops'. The site is now a housing estate. (5 July 1964)

Class '5101' No 5153 stands in the yard at Kidderminster. In the background the semaphore signal is on the Bewdley line, which is now part of the Severn Valley Railway. I cannot trace any other shed having a 'P' suffix, so does that make the shedplate more desirable and valuable? (5 July 1964)

Below: This is a nice view of the northern end of the 12-road Aston shed, whose primary duties were freight haulage. On show are Class 5MT No 45180 together with two other 'Black Fives', Nos 45114 and 45101 and Class 8F No 48762. Three of these locomotives outlasted Aston shed, which closed on 11 October 1965. (5 July 1964)

Above: Parked on the end shed road at Aston, and next to the coaling plant and the ash disposal facility, is 'Jubilee' Class No 45595 sporting the crested nameplates of *Southern Rhodesia*. The name Rhodesia is a derivative and in honour of Cecil Rhodes, who was the Prime Minister and the founder of the De Beers Mining Company in Rhodesia. In 1965 the country gained independence and in 1980 became known as Zimbabwe under Robert Mugabe's regime. I heard that Mugabe was actually from Yorkshire because his name pronounced backwards is 'e ba gum'! (5 July 1964)

9 • The Leeds area

Leeds, located in West Yorkshire, was traditionally a major centre for the wool and linen trade and was consequently an important mill town, but times have changed and it is now the largest legal and financial centre outside London.

The 1960s to the early 1970s were the golden years for football in the area, with Leeds United, managed by Don Revie, winning many trophies – but along the way earning the nickname 'Dirty Leeds', mainly because of the team's hard-tackling players, such as Billy Bremner, Norman Hunter, Jack Charlton and Johnny Giles. Some 50-odd years later, rival fans still call them 'Dirty Leeds', and I don't think they will ever lose that tag!

Leeds had two stations. Central was a terminus station, but closed in 1967 when everything was moved to the City station, which is now the third busiest rail station in the UK outside London, with 30 million passengers a year using its 17 platforms. In the early days when we visited Leeds the only two sheds we went to and 'bunked' were Neville Hill and Holbeck; for some unknown reason we never attempted Stourton, Copley Hill or Farnley Junction. However, later, on a Warwickshire Railway Society visit with a permit in 1964, these were included, but by then their allocations were diminished to the extent that on the three sheds there were only 48 locos, but I still achieved a 50% 'cop' rate.

Standing side-by-side in Neville Hill are Class 'K1' No 62028 and Class 5MT No 45204. This was originally a four-roundhouse shed until the 1950s, when two were demolished. The remaining two were given a facelift and a new building was commissioned to house and service DMUs. (29 July 1964)

Left: The last locomotive to be built at Stratford Works, London, in 1924 was Class 'N7' No 69621, and here she is with 'GER' superimposed on the British Railways logo. Withdrawal from service came in September 1962 and she was purchased privately by Middleton Railway Trust Chairman Fred Youell. She then spent a few years in store here at Neville Hill together with a few others earmarked for preservation. (29 July 1964)

Below: Out in the yard at Neville Hill with a background of semaphore signals, a carriage and an English Electric Type 3 diesel is Vincent Raven Class 'Q6' No 63420 on her home shed. She spent four years here until transferred to Normanton, then Tyne Dock, being eventually withdrawn in February 1967. (29 July 1964)

One young lad's later trainspotting trips

Above: Out in the yards at Neville Hill in a sedentary pose is Class 'A1' No 60118 *Archibald Sturrock*, also at her home shed. A week after this shot she entered Darlington Works for repair on a fractured cylinder, then lasted another year before being finally broken up by T. W. Ward at Beighton. (29 July 1964)

Left: Reallocated to Neville Hill from York the previous month, Class 'K1' No 62007 is in the yard with DMUs in the background on what were on the approaches to the service depot. This particular Peppercorn engine was only in service for 18 years before she was scrapped in 1967, but as Jim Reeves was singing in July, *I Won't Forget You.* (29 July 1964)

The Leeds area

Western Australia is bounded by Northern Territory, South Australia and the ocean, but this *Western Australia*, 'Jubilee' Class No 45568, is bounded by Sulzer Type 2 No D5234 and carriages. She is devoid of nameplates and is already withdrawn and stands in a sorry state at Holbeck shed. (29 July 1964)

In much better condition is sister 'Jubilee' No 45675 *Hardy*. She lived up to her name, being a 'hardy' member of the class with a service life of nearly 32 years, and a Holbeck (55A) engine since 1948. Just behind *Hardy* is our unofficial entrance into the shed, fully described in the next caption! (29 July 1964)

The Leeds area

Right: Holbeck always contained a mixture of LNER and LMS engines, and here we see one from each, Class 'A3' No 60038 *Firdaussi* and an unidentified 'Black Five'. The shed has much changed today, but the three-storey office block in the background, which was the main entrance to the shed on Nineveh Road, is still there as the main entrance, but under the new management of Network Rail. We entered the shed on this occasion by climbing the railway embankment (at the opposite end to this view) off Sweet Street, crossing the main lines and dropping into the shed – all dodgy stuff in those days. But to quote Will Smith from the film *After Earth*, 'Danger is very real but fear is a choice!' (1960)

Left: I'm not sure if the 'Not to be moved sign' is referring to 'Jubilee' Class No 45658 *Keyes* or the fitter seated cross-legged on the running plate – both are motionless in Holbeck! Everything looks in place – wheels, coupling rods and a boiler that has recently been cleaned out with traces of ash on the front buffer beam as evidence – so I would think she is at the end of her repair. (29 July 1964)

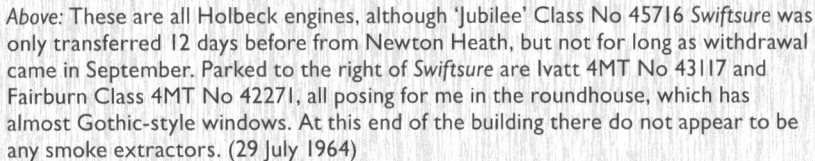

Above: These are all Holbeck engines, although 'Jubilee' Class No 45716 *Swiftsure* was only transferred 12 days before from Newton Heath, but not for long as withdrawal came in September. Parked to the right of *Swiftsure* are Ivatt 4MT No 43117 and Fairburn Class 4MT No 42271, all posing for me in the roundhouse, which has almost Gothic-style windows. At this end of the building there do not appear to be any smoke extractors. (29 July 1964)

Above right: Still at the murky end of the Holbeck roundhouses are Class 4F No 43871, 'Black Five' No 45063, 8F No 48283 and, just poking her nose in, another 4F, No 44240. The turntable locating points for each of the radiating tracks are visible in the surrounding brickwork. (29 July 1964)

Right: In the yard at Wakefield is Class 'B1' No 61131; although she carries no shedplate, she is one of the shed's 14 'B1s'. Nearly all of Wakefield's allocation were freight locos servicing National Coal Board mines. At the weekend the shed would be full as workings were fewer – maybe everybody was watching Rugby League and listening to Eddie Waring! (29 July 1964)

The Leeds area

'WD' Class No 90279 passes the site of the former Lancashire & Yorkshire Railway shed at Wakefield. If you wanted to spot 'WDs' this was an ideal shed for you, with an allocation of 57 of the class; ironically this wasn't one of them, as she was from just down the road at Doncaster. (29 July 1964)

Left: In the carriage sidings at 56C Copley Hill is Fowler Class 4MT No 42317. There were only 12 engines on shed and the end was in sight. Once having an allocation of 15 'Pacifics', we only saw two and they were tucked away inside the shed, too dark for any photos. (29 July 1964)

Right: With the Beatles dominating the Billboard Year-End Hot 100 Singles of 1964 with nine entries, over at 55B Stourton the BR 'Standard' Class 3MTs were the dominant force, but with a much lower number of four, one of them being No 77014. A class of 20 introduced by Riddles in 1954, all of them served in the Leeds area and Scotland and all were withdrawn from those areas except No 77014; for some reason the last 17 months of her life were spent on the Southern Region at Guildford, being withdrawn from there in July 1967, followed by a trip to Birds of Risca for cutting up in December. (29 July 1964)

Fairburn Class 4MT 2-6-4 tank No 42055, built at Derby in 1950, had resided at Ardsley (56B) for the last year, having been transferred from Scotland. She is just about to be boarded by one of the crew for the next duty, likely to be a local passenger service from Wakefield. (29 July 1964)

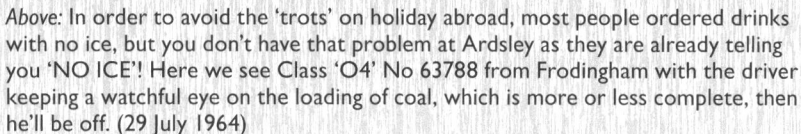

Above: In order to avoid the 'trots' on holiday abroad, most people ordered drinks with no ice, but you don't have that problem at Ardsley as they are already telling you 'NO ICE'! Here we see Class 'O4' No 63788 from Frodingham with the driver keeping a watchful eye on the loading of coal, which is more or less complete, then he'll be off. (29 July 1964)

Above right: With no prior arrangement Class 4F No 44431, hauling a full coal train, emits a nice amount of contrasting black smoke while passing us standing outside Mirfield shed. She's heading towards Bradley Wood Junction, then to either Huddersfield or Sowerby Bridge, but with the smoke drifting back to Mirfield station. (29 July 1964)

Right: 'Crab' No 42845 is on the same stretch of line at Mirfield but hauling what looks like empty coal wagons. Note the dry-stone wall running parallel to the track and an early electric streetlight seemingly in the middle of nowhere! (29 July 1964)

During an early-morning visit to Farnley Junction the mist is blocking out the sun but is not thick enough to obscure the vision of the clean lines of 'Jubilee' Class No 45562 *Alberta*, although in black and white you can see the difference in colour between the black smokebox and the green boiler and cab. (29 July 1964)

If 'Trigger' – Roger Lloyd Pack – in *Only Fools and Horses* was here this would be 'Hi Dave!' But this really is *Rodney* in the guise of 'Jubilee' Class No 45643 in the yards at Farnley Junction. (29 July 1964)

Inside 56F Low Moor there's perfect light for me to capture the fine lines of Class 'B1' No 61014 *Oribi*. This now was her home shed from the previous month, but she eventually moved to North Blyth in August 1966 and was withdrawn from there some four months later. (29 July 1964)

The Fairburn Class 4MT 2-6-4 tanks were a development of the earlier 1927 Fowler design, and this is No 42093, one of Brighton's 1951-built batch, posing outside the coaling plant of 55F Bradford Manningham. These locos were mainly used on passenger duties and No 42093 would have performed regularly on the roughly hourly service between Bradford Forster Square and Leeds City and return, with no requirement to be turned, running bunker-first on one of the legs. (29 July 1964)

Index

Locations

Ardsley shed 122
Aston shed 111
Barry 24-25; scrapyard 28-34; shed 26-27
Bescot 99
Bolton shed 56-59
Bradford Manningham shed 126
Cardiff East Dock 48-51
Cashmore's, Newport 45-48
Consett shed 78
Copley Hill shed 120
Corkerhill shed 66
Court Sart shed 83-86
Dawlish 20-23
Dawsholm shed 68
Eastfield shed 60-64
Ebbw Junction 43-45
Farnley Junction shed 123-124
Gorton 53
Heaton shed 73-75
Holbeck shed 115-118
Kidderminster shed 109-110
Kipps shed 67
Landore shed 92-93
Llantrisant shed 88-90
Low Moor shed 125
Manchester Central 52
Mirfield shed 122
Motherwell shed 68-70
Neville Hill shed 112-114
Newport shed 41-43
Newton Abbot 1, 2, 7-10
North Blyth shed 75-76
Nuneaton shed 100-102
Oxley shed 102-105
Paignton 14-17
Polmadie shed 64-66
St Rollox shed 67
Saltley shed 97-98
Severn Tunnel Junction and shed 35-40
South Blyth shed 77
Stockport Edgeley shed 53-56
Stourbridge shed 106-108
Stourton shed 120-121
Sunderland shed 79-82
Teignmouth 17-19
Tondu 91
Torquay 12-13
Tyne Dock shed 71-72
Tyseley shed 94-97
Wakefield shed 118-119

Locomotives, diesel

Type 1 ('Clayton') 70
Type 2 (North British) 2, 9, 11
Type 2 (Sulzer) 101
Type 3 ('Hymek') 12, 17, 92
Type 3 (EE) 87, 92, 93
Type 4 ('Warship') 1, 10, 12, 13, 16, 18, 19, 20, 21, 22, 23
Type 4 ('Western') 24, 92, 93
Type 4 (Brush) 97

Units, diesel

'Blue Pullman' 96

Locomotives, steam

0F 0-4-0ST (CR 'Pug') 67
'1400' 0-4-2T 91
'2251' 0-6-0 37
'2800' 2-8-0 31, 42, 44, 50, 106
2F 0-6-0 (LMS dock tank) 56
2MT 2-6-2 (BR) 58
3F 0-6-0 (CR) 61, 69
3F 0-6-0T (CR) 69
3MT 2-6-0 (BR) 120
'4200' 2-8-0T 41, 43, 48, 49, 83, 90, 91
'4500' 2-6-2T 30, 47, 95
'4575' 2-6-2T 30
'4700' 2-8-0 8
4F 0-6-0 (LMS) 53, 118, 122
4MT 2-6-0 (LMS) 99, 118
4MT 2-6-4T (BR) 60
4MT 2-6-4T (LMS) 52, 64, 105, 120, 121, 126
'5101' 2-6-2T 36, 45, 107, 110
'5205' 2-8-0T 30, 34, 43, 50
'5600' 0-6-2T 24, 27, 107
'5700' 0-6-0PT 41, 44, 84, 85, 86, 88, 89, 94, 109
5MT 2-6-0 ('Crab') 57, 59, 62, 122
5MT 4-6-0 (BR) 66, 108
5MT 4-6-0 (LMS 'Black Five') 58, 64, 67, 68, 69, 101, 103, 111, 112, 117, 118
'7200' 2-8-2T 26
'7400' 0-6-0PT 108
7F (S&D) 2-8-0 33
8F 2-8-0 39, 54, 97, 99, 101, 106, 111, 118
'9400' 0-6-0T 25
9F 2-10-0 19, 38, 40, 45, 50, 72, 94, 97, 107
'A1' 4-6-2 66, 114
'A3' 4-6-2 62, 74, 75, 117
'A4' 4-6-2 73
'B1' 4-6-0 60, 97, 118, 125
'Britannia' 4-6-2 102, 103
'Castle' 4-6-0 31, 43, 44, 45, 46, 51, 94, 95, 102, 103, 108
'Coronation' 4-6-2 64
'County' 4-6-0 46, 48
'G2A' 0-8-0 99
'Grange' 4-6-0 25, 42, 104, 106
'Hall' 4-6-2 7, 10, 11, 12, 14, 17, 20, 21, 32, 42, 44, 95, 97, 104, 108
'J27' 0-6-0 75, 76, 77, 79, 82
'J72' 0-6-0 72, 73
'Jubilee' 4-6-0 54, 56, 57, 68, 111, 115, 116, 117, 118, 123, 124
'K1' 2-6-0 78, 81, 112, 114
'King' 4-6-0 32
'Manor' 4-6-0 104
'N7' 0-6-2T 113
'O4' 2-8-0 122
'Q6' 0-8-0 71, 72, 78, 80, 82, 113
'Royal Scot' 4-6-0 65, 66, 67
'V2' 2-6-2 63, 73
'V3' 2-6-2T 75, 77
WD 0-6-0ST 29
WD 2-8-0 55, 119

Silver Link Silk Editions

In March 2014 we introduced the first of our Silver Link Silk Editions, which will feature a silver, gold or green silk style bookmark (the use of such silks dates back to the reign of Elizabeth I). Printed on high quality gloss art paper, these sewn hardcover volumes also feature head and tail bands. Such quality and tradition will be much welcomed by today's discerning print book readers.

Further Silk Edition volumes will be made available from time to time and details will be shown on our web site:

www.nostalgiacollection.com

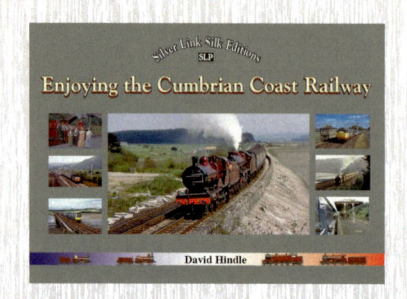

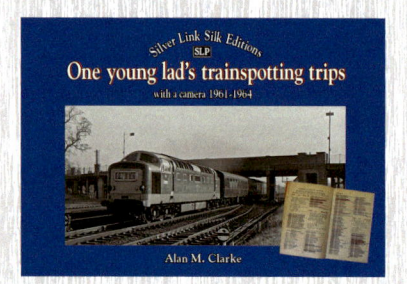

Further information

Silver Link and Past & Present titles are available while stocks last through bookshops, preserved railways and many heritage sites throughout the UK.

Further details can be found on our web site:

www.nostalgiacollection.com

Our latest catalogue is also available on request by writing to us at the address shown on the title page of this volume or by emailing your request to:

sohara@mortons.co.uk

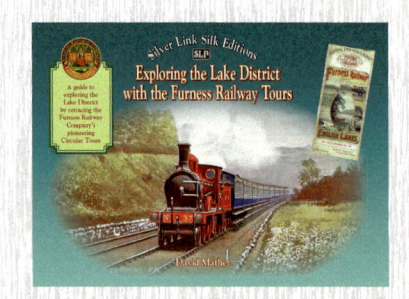

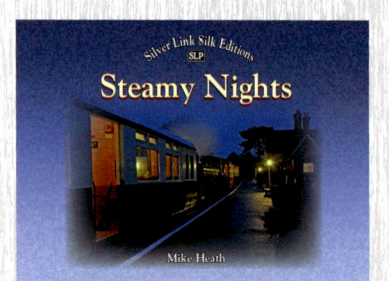

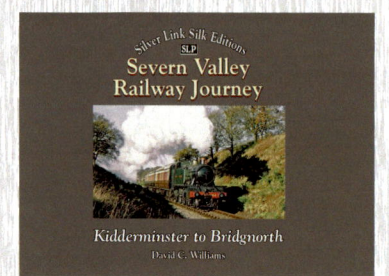

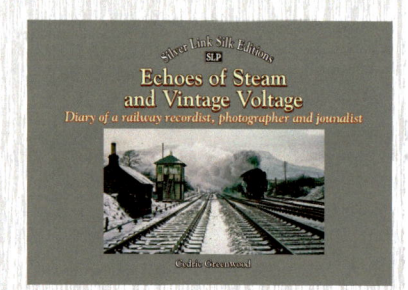